Frank Vincent

The land of the white elephant

Sights and scenes in south-eastern Asia

Frank Vincent

The land of the white elephant
Sights and scenes in south-eastern Asia

ISBN/EAN: 9783741143120

Manufactured in Europe, USA, Canada, Australia, Japa

Cover: Foto ©Andreas Hilbeck / pixelio.de

Manufactured and distributed by brebook publishing software (www.brebook.com)

Frank Vincent

The land of the white elephant

ANGKOR WAT. PRINCIPAL FAÇADE.

THE LAND

OF THE

WHITE ELEPHANT

SIGHTS and SCENES in SOUTH-EASTERN ASIA

A PERSONAL NARRATIVE OF TRAVEL AND ADVENTURE

IN

FARTHER INDIA

EMBRACING THE COUNTRIES OF

BURMA, SIAM, CAMBODIA, AND COCHIN-CHINA

(1871-2)

BY FRANK VINCENT, JUN.

WITH MAP, PLANS, AND NUMEROUS ILLUSTRATIONS

LONDON
SAMPSON LOW, MARSTON, LOW, & SEARLE
CROWN BUILDINGS, 188 FLEET STREET
1873

All rights reserved

LONDON: PRINTED BY
SPOTTISWOODE AND CO., NEW-STREET SQUARE
AND PARLIAMENT STREET

TO

BARON HENRY CALICÉ

MINISTER-RESIDENT AND CONSUL-GENERAL OF

HIS I. AND R. AP. M. THE EMPEROR OF AUSTRIA, KING OF HUNGARY, ETC.

IN CHINA, JAPAN, AND SIAM

.

WITH PLEASANT REMEMBRANCE OF RARE EXPERIENCES IN

SHANGHAI, CHEFOO, AND PEKING

This Volume

DESCRIPTIVE OF THE PEOPLES AND COUNTRIES OF INDO-CHINA

Is Gratefully Inscribed

PREFACE

WITHIN the past five years the attention of the western world especially has been earnestly and anxiously directed to many of the countries of Asia — to Burma, Siam, Cambodia, and Cochin China amongst others—where unusual and extraordinary innovations have been introduced, where encouraging social and religious revolutions have been initiated, and where 'modern progress' is now so rapid as almost to raise fears of dangerous reaction or even collapse.

Last year the Kings of Siam and Cambodia left, for the first time in history, their capital cities, and travelled in search of instruction and pleasure, the one to Java and India and the other to Hong Kong and Peking.

Opinions, laws, customs, even religions, which have been rooted and established for ages, are gradually undergoing change, and a change on the whole for the better. And still there are no countries in Asia, where the arts of civilised life are understood, of which we have so limited a knowledge as those which lie between the Bay of Bengal and the China

Sea. Although during the present century something has been learned, yet much remains to be told; a great deal of important information has to be gathered before we can claim a full and true acquaintance with the kingdoms and protectorates of Farther India—their present condition, capabilities, and prospects. A country of 1,000,000 square miles in area and 25,000,000 inhabitants—having a wonderfully productive soil and a greatly extended commerce — with which the unavoidable march of events shows we are soon to have more intimate relations, certainly merits a careful study.

A three-years' journey round the world—the greater part of the time occupied in which was employed in studying Man and Nature in the various lands of southern and eastern Asia (from Persia to Tibet, to Mongolia and Japan) and but recently completed—included visits to Farther India or Indo-China (as it is also styled) in the years 1871-72. The following pages also contain a personal narrative of travel and adventure in Burma, Siam, Cambodia, and Cochin China, for which little else is claimed than the merit of being true.

F. V. Jr.

CONTENTS

BURMA

CHAPTER I
RANGOON

Steamer 'Oriental'—Glances at Indian Towns—First View of Land—Approach to Burma—Shipping—The Rangoon River—Rangoon City—Arrival—Search for Quarters—Historical—Description of the City—Population—The *Shway Dagon*, or Golden Pagoda—Temples—Great Bell of Rangoon—Its Inscription—Generous Treatment—Other Pagodas . . . page 1

CHAPTER II
BURMESE MANNERS AND CUSTOMS

The Burman Race—Ethnology—Houses—Dress—Tattooing—Food—Infant Smokers—Jewellery—The Oath of a Witness in Court—Language and Literature—Religion—Leave Rangoon for Mandalay 11

CHAPTER III
UP THE IRRAWADDY

The 'Colonel Phayre' and 'Pegu'—My Fellow-Passengers—The Irrawaddy River—Scenery—Myanoung—Budhist Idols—Market—'Arakan Hills'—River Boats, Canoes, and Cargoes—Burmese Characteristics—The 'Marriage-knot'—Prome—'All Quiet at the Capital'—A Royal Religious Gift—Mergla 21

CHAPTER IV

PAGHAN AND THE OLD CAPITALS

The Kingdom of Ava—Yaynan-gyoung—Petroleum Wells—Ruins of Paghan—Counterpart of an English Archbishop of the Middle Ages—Large Pagoda of Indian Model—Ava—Amarapoora—Changes of Capital—The 'Golden City' at last . . . . page 31

CHAPTER V

MANDALAY

The Landing—Great Bell of Mengoon—Mr. Seng-Ko's Letter—First View of the City—The Suburbs—Roads—Fires—Chinese Dwellings—Population—The City—Walls; Gates; Streets; Canals—The Palace Walls—Royal Guards—The *Pakhen Mengyee*, or Foreign Minister—A Burmese Regiment of Infantry —Palace Square—The 'Grand Hall of Audience'—The Prime Minister's Breakfast—Conversation with the *You-Atween-Woon*, or Minister of the Interior—The 'Governor of the Glass Manufactories'—Government Accounts—The King's Throne and Audience Chamber 38

CHAPTER VI

AUDIENCE WITH THE KING OF AVA

Our Party and Presents—King Moungton Appears—The Royal Person—Presentation to His Majesty—A Spy—Tempting Offers—A Veritable 'Houri'—The King's Reign—The Government—Tyranny and Monopoly—Some Appreciation of the Advantages of Western Civilisation—Native Account of the Introduction of the Electric Telegraph 54

CHAPTER VII

THE WHITE ELEPHANT

The White Elephant, *not* White—The King 'out of sorts'—The White Elephant in the Sixteenth and Eighteenth Centuries—The White Elephant at the Present Day—His Majesty's 'Pass'—Writing Material and Books—A Burma-Chinese Tiffin—Odd Use of Tea Leaves—The Bazaars—Coins; Interest; Barter; Prices—The Market—The Royal Navy—The King's Barge. 63

CHAPTER VIII

BHAMO AND THE OLD TRADE ROUTE

Leaving Mandalay—The Upper Irrawaddy—Domesticated Fish—Grand Defile—Mineral and Vegetable Resources of Ava—Old Trade Route to China—By Rail to the Makong River—Bhamo—Shan Emigrants—The Laos Tribes—The Hide Trade—Our Cargo—The English Cantonment at Thayet-myo—General Norman and Secretary Seward—Change of Monsoon—Proposed Overland Trip to Bangkok—Prome Again—Arrival at Rangoon . . . page 74

CHAPTER IX

FROM MAULMAIN AND PENANG

Amherst—Maulmain—Timber Yards—Sagacity and Usefulness of the Elephant—Departure for Penang—Chinese Passengers; their Life on Board—The Bishop of Rangoon, Right Rev. T. Bigandet—First View of Penang—The Island—Province Wellesley—Georgetown—General Appearance—Visit to 'Penang Mountain'—The Waterfall—The Signal Station—Magnificent View—Return to the Steamer—The Mangostoen—The Dorian—The Straits of Malacca 81

CHAPTER X

TO MALACCA AND SINGAPORE

The Town of Malacca—Chinese Burying-ground—A Portuguese Tiffin—Old Cathedral—Captain Somers' Piracy—Approach to Singapore—The Harbour—Hôtel de l'Europe'—The Island and its Products—The 'Town of Lions'—The American Consul—View from Fort Canning—The Governor's House—Chinese Temple—The Market—European Country Houses—New Harbour—Cocoanut Plantations—Coir-Rope Manufactory—Hon. Mr. Whampoa's Gardens—A Sago Manufactory 99

SIAM

CHAPTER XI
BANGKOK

A Short Digression—Steamer 'Martaban'—The Gulf of Siam—Mouth of the Menam River—Paknam—A Siamese Custom House—The River and its Scenery—The City—Consulates of the Western Powers—My Hotel—The Royal Secretary—The American Consul—A Row through the City—The Thoroughfares—Floating Houses—Boats and Canoes—Rice Factories—A Huge Pagoda—General Appearance of Bangkok—*Wat Cheng* Pagoda—Siamese Drama and Music—*Wat Sak Prak Tim*—Large Chinese Temple—A Ride to the Palace Buildings . . . . page 115

CHAPTER XII
EXCURSION TO PECHABURI

The Second King's Private Secretary—The Canal—The Country—A Royal Sanitarium—American Mission Station—The King's Summer Palace—Cave Temples—Huge Idol—The 'Reclining' Budha—A Laos Village—Return to Bangkok 133

CHAPTER XIII
AUDIENCE WITH THE KING OF SIAM

The Second King—The Consuls—The Palace—Audience with His Majesty—Personal Appearance and Character of the Second King—Cigars, Coffee, and a Pleasant Talk—Grand Parade of the Palace Guards—The Royal Military Bands—Bonzes Seeking Alms—Interview with the Regent of Siam—His Grace Chow Phya Sri Sury Wongse—The 'Real Ruler of Siam' . . . 145

CHAPTER XIV
A DAY IN THE PALACE

White Elephants—Budhist Reverence for White Quadrupeds—Sir John Bowring's Gift—Why the White Elephant is so Specially Revered—A Badge of Distinction—Two Royal Claims to the Title of 'Master of Many White Elephants'—The Arsenal of Artillery—'Coining Manufactory'—The *Wat*

Phrea Kexu; or, Temple of the Emerald Idol—Description; Exterior and Interior—Library of Budhist Sacred Books—The Supreme King's Palace—*Wat Poh*; Gigantic Image of Budha—Preparation for the Overland Excursion to Angkor—Our Official Passport—Farewell to Bangkok . . . . page 160

CHAPTER XV

ACROSS SOUTHERN SIAM

Canal Travel—Bang pa Kong River—Pachim—The Governor—Interview with His Excellency—The Citadel—Remarkable Trees—A Paddy-Mill—Horses; Bullocks; and Carts—A Siamese Dinner—Scenery of the Road—Kabin—Gold Mine—The Forest and its Wild Inhabitants—Quinine—We Pass the Boundaries of Ancient Cambodia—Our Night Bivouacs—Sempon—Siamese Elephant, Saddle, and Driver—Fish Traps—Panoum-sok—The Governor's Wife 175

CHAPTER XVI

SIAMRAP

Ancient Stone Bridge—Ride in a Bullock-Cart—A Border Town—A Marriage Festival—Another Native Dinner—Presents from the Governor—A Water-Wheel—Canoes and Barges—The Walls and Houses—The Palace—Interview with the Governor—His Excellency's Band—*Résumé* of Travel—Preparations and Start for Angkor and *Nagkon Wat* 199

CHAPTER XVII

THE RUINS OF ANGKOR; THE GREAT TEMPLE

Preliminary Observations—Description of the Great *Nagkon Wat*; Exterior and Interior—*No Cement Used in Construction*—Quarry Thirty Miles Distant—A Half a Mile of Sculptured Wall—*One Hundred Thousand Separate Figures*—Bas-Reliefs of the 'Grand Gallery'—*Fifteen Hundred Solid Columns*—Galleries, Image Houses, Pagodas—Figures of Budha—Who Built the Wonderful *Nagkon Wat*?—When was it Built?—Native Account—Its Great Antiquity Established—The Lost Tribes of Israel—Our Opinion—*Inscriptions*; Ancient and Modern—Former Cannot be Deciphered, and Latter throw no Historical Light—Chinese Discovery, and Portuguese Re-Discovery—*Nagkon Wat* from the year 1295 to 1872 209

CHAPTER XVIII

A CAMBODIAN MARRIAGE FESTIVAL

Other Ruins—Lailan—The Royal Lake, Saeoug—Visit to Siamrap—Letter from the Governor of Siamrap to the Prime Minister of Cambodia—Dinner at the Palace—Siamese and Chinese Viands Compared—Gold Betel-Boxes, Cigar-holders, Cups, and Dishes—Invitation to Accompany some Chinese Travellers to Panompin—The Marriage Festival—The Bride and Bridegroom—The Ceremony—The Grand Banquet—*Nak Prat*, the 'Wise Man'—The Governor's Idea Concerning the Builders of Angkor—The Wedding Presents—We Return to *Naghon Wat* . . . . page 225

CHAPTER XIX

THE RUINS OF ANGKOR: THE CITY AND ENVIRONS

A Visit to the Old City—Tradition of the Power and Magnificence of the Ancient Kingdom of Khaman—The Walls—Large Temple—Colossal Faces of Badha built in the Pagodas—The *Pet* Trees—Idol Cells—The Leper King—Founders of Angkor—Is the Religion of Badha Identical with that of Ancient Egypt?—Did the Egyptians build Angkor City and Temple?—Resemblance of Badhism to Christianity—The Royal Palace—Custodian of the Ruined City—Remains of an Observatory—Immense Stone Griffins—*The Elephant-headed 'General' of the Hindoo Mythology*—Image Houses—Description of the Observatory—Extensive View—An Evening Call—Parting from my Fellow-Travellers 239

———o◊o———

CAMBODIA

CHAPTER XX

SIAMRAP TO PANOMPIN

Preparations—My Cochin-China Servant—An Amusing Dinner—The Start for Lake Thalayeap—Road to the Lake—Description of our Boat—*Campong Pluk*—A Fishing Village—Vexatious Delays—A Second Start—Enter 'Sweet-

Water' Lake—Pass the Boundary of Siam and Cambodia—Boat Life in Cambodia—'Joss' on Board—The Mesap River—Villages—River Fisheries—Oudong, the Old Capital—Views on the River—Approach to Panompin . . . . page 255

CHAPTER XXI

PANOMPIN

General Appearance—Panompin from the River—An Interpreter and Friend—Description of the Capital of Cambodia—Roads; Shops; Population—Inhabitants; their Dress—Miriano, the Interpreter—The Chief Aide-de-Camp—The Prime Minister—His Reception Hall—The Palace Inclosure—Details of the Royal Palace 269

CHAPTER XXII

AUDIENCE WITH THE KING OF CAMBODIA

Norodom I.—Conversation with His Majesty—The Greatest Fête ever Celebrated—Interior of the Palace—The Drawing-room—Apartments of the Harem—Dining-room—Large Orchestral Music Box, with a Wonderful Mechanical Bird—The King's $1,000 Watch—The Library—His Majesty's Bed-room—Gold and Silver Toilet Services—Pictures—Observatory and Telescope—Reflections—The Artificial (stone, silver, and gold) Mountain—Cutting off a Princess's Hair—The King an Inveterate Smoker—Palace Guards 277

CHAPTER XXIII

WALKS ABOUT THE CITY

An Old Pagoda—Music at the Palace—Machine Shops—The King's Private Office—Ambassadors' 'Audience Hall'—Supreme Court—Royal Theatre—Barracks—His Majesty's Stables—Horses presented by Napoleon III.—Description of the Old Capital, Oudong—A Telegram from Saigon—My Last Interview with the King—The Royal Carriage and Cavalry Escort—A Royal Cambodian 'Swell:' the King in Semi-European Garb—Present of a Gold Box—The Theatricals—Our Boat and Crew—Adieu to Panompin . . . 289

COCHIN CHINA

CHAPTER XXIV

PANOMPIN TO SAIGON

The Great Mekong River—Products of the Country—Enter Cochin China—Chaudoc—Citadel and Garrison—French Justice—Lang-Xuen, Chadec, and Mitho—Intendant's Residence—French Settlement—Delta-ground of the Mekong—The Creek—Chinese Merchant-Boats—Cholen—Ride to Saigon—Ancient Annamite Tombs—Arrive at the City—Congratulations—Times and Distances of the Overland Journey from Bangkok . . . . page 298

CHAPTER XXV

SAIGON

Brief Geographical Notice—First Impressions—The River: Gunboats and Shipping—Hotels and Cafés—Population—Administration—Streets—Botanical Garden—Government House—Business—The 'Toilet of the East'—Schools for Annamites—Army and Navy—Police System—Morals—Climate: Diseases—Language—'France in the East'—Colonisation—The Mekong as a Water-Road—The Value of Cochin China—The Songkoi as a 'Back Way' to the Yang-tse-kiang—The Saigon River—Departure—Conclusion . . 306

LIST OF ILLUSTRATIONS

FULL-PAGE ENGRAVINGS

1. The Great Temple of *Nagkon Wat* . . . . . . *Frontispiece*

BURMA

2. Gaudama, the last Budha . . . . . *to face page* 8
3. Burmese Image-House 21
4. View of the City of Mandalay 38
5. Budhist Monastery 41
6. The Palace, Mandalay 44

SINGAPORE

7. The Fan Palm—'The Traveller's Fountain' . . . 109

SIAM

8. General View of Bangkok and the Menam River . . . 115
9. His Majesty the King of Siam 118
10. Temples and Pagodas at Bangkok 125
11. *Wat Chang* Pagoda, Bangkok 128
12. Brass Idol in Temple, Bangkok 130
13. Supreme King of Siam in his State Robes 132
14. The Second King of Siam in his State Robes . . . 145
15. Temple of the Emerald Idol 165
16. Siamese Gentleman and Lady 197

LIST OF ILLUSTRATIONS

RUINS OF ANGKOR

17. *Nagkon Wat*: Entrance West of the First Enceinte (inner view) to face page				209
18. „ „ North-West Edicule				210
19. „ „ Principal Façade				212
20. „ „ Peristyle of the Gallery of Bas-Reliefs				214
21. Sculptures at *Nagkon Wat*				216
22. *Nagkon Wat*: Fragment of Bas-Relief				218
23. Colonnade at *Nagkon Wat*				220
24. The Grand Staircase, *Nagkon Wat*				220
25. View from Central Pagoda, *Nagkon Wat*				224
26. Angle of the Great Court of the Temple				227

CAMBODIA

27. His Majesty the King of Cambodia	277
28. Queen of Cambodia and Royal Children	283
29. Panompin, the Capital of Cambodia	289

COCHIN CHINA

30. Cochin Chinese Prince and Attendants	299
31. Street View, Saigon	306
32. Government House, Saigon (French, recently completed)	308
33. Annamite Lady	310

SMALLER ENGRAVINGS

	Page
1. Burmese Woman	13
2. Burmese Judge, Clerks, and Attendants	17
3. Copy of an Old Burmese Painting	19
4. Irrawaddy River-Boat	23

LIST OF ILLUSTRATIONS xix

	PAGE
5. Elephant employed in a Timber-Yard, Maulmain	86
6. A Bodhist Priest	89
7. Temple of the Sleeping Idol, Bangkok	128
8. The Royal Guards	132
9. The Regent of Siam	135
10. The Minister of Foreign Affairs	157
11. Siamese War-Elephant	195
12. Cambodian Female Band	207
13. Priest's House, Nagkon Wat	211
14. Sculptures in the City of Angkor	214
15. Columns of Nagkon Wat	217
16. Wooden Idol	241
17. The Leper King	243
18. Banks of the River Mesap, Cambodia	266
19. Annamite Female	287
20. Gift from the King of Cambodia	295
21. Makong River-Boats	304
22. Annamite Male	309
23. Annamite Soldiers	311

MAP AND PLANS

Sketch Map of the Author's Route.
Plan of the Province of Siamrap; showing the location of the Ruins of Angkor.
Ground Plan of the Great Nagkon Wat, in Eastern Siam.

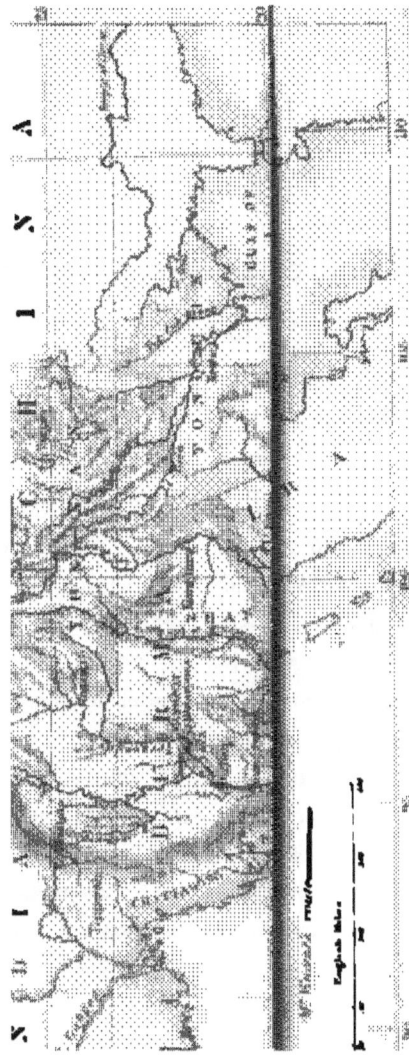

THE LAND
OF
THE WHITE ELEPHANT

CHAPTER I.

RANGOON

It was at daybreak on the 2nd of April, 1871, that we—an English friend was with me—first saw the shores of Burma. We had been a short time at sea, having left Madras eight days previously, but the end of the voyage was none the less welcome, for it was about the season that the monsoon changes, and those terrific revolving storms called cyclones sweep the upper part of the Bay of Bengal, so often with fatal effect. Our steamer was the 'Oriental' (Capt. Smith). We had a full list of passengers, many of them being English officers, who were ordered from various Indian stations to the cantonment of Toungoo, on the Sittang river, in north-eastern Burma. The route usually taken by these steamers—calling at Masulipatam, Coconada, Vizagapatam, and Bimlipatam on the coast of India, and thence nearly due east to Rangoon—is about a thousand miles in length.

We enjoyed a remarkably pleasant voyage. Masulipatam was reached on the second day. This town is of importance only as being the nearest seaport to the large city of Secunderabad, in the Nizam's dominions of Southern India. In 1865 a tremendous cyclone and tidal wave destroyed thirty thousand of the inhabitants, and nearly all the buildings of the town. Coconada is a larger town than Masulipatam, and from it are exported large quantities of cotton, castor-oil, seeds, and grain. On the third day we anchored off Vizagapatam, a large town, most picturesquely situated on a plain surrounded by gently sloping hills, near the sea shore. The houses are built of mud and unburnt bricks; and crowning the summits of several of the nearer hills are graceful little temples; and at their bases date and cocoa palms, whose green, feathery leaves add very much to the beauty of the scene. Leaving Bimlipatam—a simple cluster of mud huts—we saw nothing but sky and water until the lighthouse on the Alguada reef, fifteen or twenty miles distant from Cape

Negrais (the south-west extremity of Pegu), rose up from the ocean's bed before us. It is erected on a very dangerous reef, more than a mile in length, and much of which is only just above water at low tide. The shaft, built of a red stone, is 160 feet in height, and, no land being in sight, certainly presented a most singular appearance; however, with our binoculars we could distinguish two or three lines of billows dashing themselves one after another upon the dark rocks.

Soon after 'sighting' the land we received on board the pilot, and then half an hour's steaming brought us to the mouth of the Rangoon river, with its low, wooded shores, and red obelisks on either headland—warnings to the mariner. Sandbanks, whose edges are marked by large iron buoys indicating the channel's bed, stretched for a long distance out to sea. We passed a dozen or more large ships before reaching the river's mouth; these, the captain informed us, anchored there in order to free themselves from the port dues to which they would be subject if lying at the city, and the masters go 'up to town' and engage their cargoes. At its entrance the Rangoon river is two miles in width, while opposite the city, twenty-six miles above, it narrows to about a third of a mile, with four or five fathoms' depth. The foreign ships anchored in the river made a very considerable show, our visit being at the height of the rice season. Rangoon, lying upon level ground, extends for about a mile along the river, and perhaps three times that distance inland. By the bank of the river there runs a broad macadamised street, called 'the Strand,' and facing this are the Government offices and many imposing and substantial stores and dwelling-houses. The city abounds with rich tropical foliage, which shades many of the teak and bamboo built huts, and from the steamer's deck we can see a small English cantonment, two or three European churches, and several large pagodas, with gilded and richly ornamented spires. Beyond the city we see a jungle of palms and bananas, and bamboos stretching away, a waving sea of green, to the very horizon itself. The country about Rangoon—the delta of the great Irrawaddy river—is of much the same nature as that at the *embouchure* of the Ganges, being low, sandy, and muddy, and subject to tremendous floods in the rainy season.

There are two or three hotels in Rangoon, but these were full, and not being able to obtain rooms in any private dwelling, we were compelled 'to go to housekeeping,' i.e. to have an entire cottage and order our meals from a neighbouring bakery. The next few days were pleasantly passed in seeing 'the sights' of the city.

Rangoon, the commercial capital of Burma, was founded by King Alompra, the Burmese conqueror of Pegu, in 1755, and was peopled by the inhabitants of the ancient capital of the province, who were brought away for that purpose. It was captured by the British during the first Burmese war in 1824, but was afterwards restored. In 1852 it again fell into the hands of the English, and will now remain, doubtless, permanently in their possession. The population at present is about 60,000—Burmese, Chinese, and Hindoos. The streets of Rangoon are laid out at right angles, and most of them are broad, macadamised, and clean. The greater part of the European private residences are raised upon piles. These are built of plain teak boards and have tiled roofs, but the native town or quarter is very mean-looking, the huts there being of bamboo, with palm-leaf thatched covers.

The most wonderful sight in Rangoon is the great *Shoay Dagon*, or Golden Pagoda—the largest edifice of the kind in Burma, and probably the largest in the world. It is situated about a mile from the city upon a hill perhaps eighty or a hundred feet in height. The entrance, guarded by two huge griffins of brick and mortar, passes between long narrow sheds, which are beautifully carved and gaudily painted in vermilion and gold, and covered with horrid representations of the Budhistic tortures reserved for the damned; and thence, mounting a very dilapidated staircase, the immense stone terrace upon which the pagoda itself stands is reached. This terrace is nearly a thousand feet square, and the base of the structure, standing at its centre, is octagonal-shaped and fifteen hundred feet in circumference, while the entire height of the pagoda is three hundred feet. It is built of solid masonry and lime, covered with gold leaf, and gradually tapers to a spire, which terminates in a *tee* (umbrella), an open iron-work cap, twenty-six feet in height. The gold upon this pagoda is said to equal the weight of a former Burmese king, and the spire blazes so fiercely under a noonday's sun as to almost dazzle the beholder. At the base of the immense structure are broad stone steps and large griffins, and also some smaller pagodas of like design and finish.

Within the enclosure of the pagoda are many temples, most of them containing huge images of Gaudama (the last Budha), made of wood, brick and lime, marble and metal, and nearly all thickly gilded; some of the sitting figures are twelve feet, and some of

GAUDAMA, THE LAST BUDHA

the standing ones as much as eighteen feet in height. I noticed that all the faces wore a humorous, contented expression, one sensual, however, rather than intellectual. Some of their drapery was made of minute pieces of glass, especially were the fringes of the robes thus ornamented. This gave them the appearance of coats of mail, and when different coloured glasses were used in a court dress the effect was quite gay. Some of the idols were clothed in yellow garments—yellow being the ordained colour of all priestly robes. On small tables in front of many of the images were placed candles, flowers, and little paper flags; some of these being used in the forms of worship, and some having been presented as offerings by religious devotees. Lofty poles were planted at short intervals around the pagoda. These were crowned with *tees*, and also at several feet from their tops were fixed rudely made game-cocks—the national emblem of the Burmese—and the remainder of the pole was hung with varicoloured streamers. Burma is well known to be one of the strongholds of Budhism. The *Shoay Dagon* pagoda derives its peculiar sanctity from being the depository, according to Burmese tradition, of relics of the last four Budhas — viz. the staff of Kanthathon, the water-dipper of Gaunagon, a garment of Kathapa, and eight hairs from the head of Gaudama. Burman pagodas, it may be observed, are not temples, but monuments erected to the memory of Gaudama, and they are all supposed to contain sacred relics, and consequently are objects of worship to the Budhist. The Golden Pagoda rears its lofty head from a beautiful grove of Palmyra and cocoa palms and mango trees, but it is not a very symmetrical structure, the base being far too large and the shaft too massive to secure an elegant effect.

What is justly termed 'the great bell' of Rangoon is hung in a gaily ornamented pavilion near the large pagoda. I stood upright under it with perfect ease, and a dozen men might have stood there with me. The bell has a long inscription in the Burman character, eulogistic of the king who presented it, cut around its circumference. Hopes are expressed that for this meritorious gift, replete with the virtue of beneficence, he (the king who presented the bell) may be conducted to Nieban (the Budhist heaven), and obtain the destined blessing of men, *nats* (genii), and Brahmas by means of divine perfection, and that he may also obtain in his transmigration only the regal state among men and *nats*. 'Thus, in order to cause the voice of homage during the period of five hundred years to be heard at the monument of the divine hair in the city of Rangoon, let the reward of the great merit of giving the great bell called Maha Gauda be unto the royal mother queen, the royal father proprietor of life, lord of the white elephant, the royal grandfather Aloungmeng, the royal uncle, the royal aunt-queen, the royal sons, the royal daughters, the royal relatives, the royal concubines, the noblemen, the military officers, and teachers. Let the nats who guard the religious dispensation five thousand years; the nats who guard the royal city, palace, and umbrella; the nats who all around guard the empire, the provinces, and villages; the nats who guard the monuments of the divine hair, around the hill Tampakokta, together with the nats governing Bomma and Akatho, and all rational beings throughout the universe, utter praises and accept the supplications.'

Though many natives were in the pagoda enclosure, we were allowed to freely walk about, to enter all the image-houses, and to inspect everything at our leisure, the Burmese having less fanatical notions in regard to their religious edifices than either the Hindoos or Mohammedans. The English military officials have built a strong brick wall, pierced for musketry, about the Golden Pagoda, to serve as a temporary retreat in case of any sudden outbreak among the natives, and because it, being upon high ground, commands the city, and the cantonments are near at hand.

There are several other smaller pagodas in Rangoon, but all of them are built pretty much on the same plan; the base consists of one or more quadrangles, succeeded by a tapering bell-shaped structure, either round or forming a polygon, the apex of which is crowned with the *tee* (umbrella), and without that addition it would be considered incomplete. The building itself is invariably a solid mass of masonry constructed of unburnt brick, with an outer coating of plaster, which usually is richly gilded.

CHAPTER II.

BURMESE MANNERS AND CUSTOMS

It is now generally believed that the Burmese, and indeed all the various races and nations of Indo-China, migrated at a remote period from the plateaus of Central Asia, and that they are of mixed origin, possessing some of the characteristics of the Hindoo (the Caucasian) and some also of the Chinaman (the Mongol). Thus in person they are short and stout, with the small, oblique eyes, high and prominent cheekbones, and flat, short, and broad nose of the Tartar, Chinese, and Japanese races, and the 'raven black' hair, pearly teeth, and olive-brown skin of the Hindoos and the Malays; and though of nearly the same stature as the latter, they generally possess the stouter frames of the former. The Burmese are a simple-minded, indolent people, frank and courteous, fond of amusement and gay-coloured apparel, friendly among themselves and hospitable to strangers. They appreciate a quiet life, smoking, and gossiping, and sleeping throughout the day, and listening to wild music and singing through half of the night; 'stern' ambition is among them, indeed, a very rare trait of character.

Burmese houses are built of teak wood, palm leaf, bamboo, rattan, and grass; and are generally raised upon piles four or five feet from the ground, as a preservative against fevers, bred by the great dampness of the climate, and to provide against the inundations of the rainy season. Native villages often consist of but one long and broad street, running through perfect jungles of date, banana, palm, or other tropical trees; and beneath and among these, nearly concealed from view, are the little bamboo huts, artfully carved monasteries, and tapering pagodas.

The costume of the Burmese is remarkably simple. Both sexes wear a short white jacket, called an *engie*; and the male a *putso* (a piece of silk or cotton cloth, usually the former), and of gay colour (red or yellow), about a yard in width, and four or five in length, which is worn round the hips; while the women wear a *tentine*, which is a nearly square piece of cloth, or silk, sufficiently large to wrap around the body, but fastened merely by tucking the outer end within the other, and consequently it gapes open at every step taken by the wearer, and discloses nearly the whole of one leg; but this exhibition, being 'the custom,' is not deemed immodest. The men wear gay-coloured silk bandannas—*gounboungs*—in adjusting which they sometimes entwist a thick lock of hair; the women wear no

BURMESE WOMAN

head covering. Both men and women leave their hair long; the former gather it in a bunch on the top of their head, and the latter comb it straight back from the forehead and tie it in a knot on the back of the head. The men seldom or never wear any hair upon their faces, unless it might be a very feeble moustache. The sexes generally walk barefooted, though the women sometimes wear a sort of leather sandal, made after the classical Roman model.

The Burmese males are all tattooed from above the hips to the knees with a blackish-blue pigment, and some besides have punctured spots upon the upper part of the body stained a vermilion colour. This tattooing of the thighs is a painful operation; it is done when they are very young, a little at a time, and opium is often administered on such occasions, and deaths from an overdose of this drug, or from inflammation, are not infrequent. Regarding this curious custom of tattooing the body of the males, and of the immodest dress of the females, an old traveller in Burma states that, 'the men of this nation have a singular custom of tattooing their thighs, which is done by wounding the skin and then filling the wound with the juice of certain plants, which has the property of producing a black stain. Some, besides both their thighs, will also stain their legs of the same colours, and others paint them all over with representations of tigers, cats, and other animals. The origin of this custom, as well as of the immodest dress of the women, is said to have been the policy of a certain queen, who, observing that the men were deserting their wives and giving themselves up to abominable vices, persuaded her husband to establish these customs by a royal order, that thus by disfiguring the men, and setting off the beauty of the women, the latter might regain the affections of their husbands.'

The food of the Burmese is both simple and wholesome. The general food of the nations of southern and eastern Asia is rice. Of the Burmese we may say that salt fish, rice and *ngapee*, and fruits constitute the solid and substantial part of their bill of fare, while betel-nut and the cheroot make quite an enjoyable dessert. The condiment *ngapee*, for which there is a very great demand, is made of preserved fish, fish which has arrived at that epicurean stage termed 'high;' it is a sort of paste which mixes with rice like the Indian sauce, *chutnee*. The betel-nut is extensively used, and most houses have about or near them trellises of the piper-betel plant, which is chewed with the nut. Smoking is universal and continual among both sexes and all ages; cheroots of solid tobacco, but more often a preparation covered with a green-leaf wrapper, and some of them of enormous size, are used. Burmese boys take to smoking even earlier than do the youths of this country. I have frequently seen babes at their mothers' breast alternating the nourishment of 'Nature's Nile' with pulls and puffs at their cheroots.

The natives of Burma do not appear to wear so much jewellery as the Hindoos, but they delight especially in ear ornaments. The lobe of the ear is bored to a hole of astonishing size—often an inch in diameter—and in it various articles are worn: pieces of wood, jewels, or rolls of solid gold or silver. When no ornaments are in the ears, the men often put their cheroots, or any small article in frequent use, through them, and the women use them as bouquet holders or flower-stands, thus presenting a very comical appearance.

Burmese laws on the whole seem wise, and evidently are calculated to advance the interests of justice and morality; but they very often prove futile, owing to the tyranny and rapacity of the king and the venality of many of his officers. False swearing is particularly obnoxious to the Burmese citizen. A witness in court takes a fearful oath, which is so singular that I give it entire, through a translation: 'I will speak the truth. If I speak not the truth, may it be through the influence of the laws of demerit—viz. passion, anger, folly, pride, false opinion, immodesty, hard-heartedness, and scepticism—so that when I and my relations are on land, land animals—as tigers, elephants, buffaloes, poisonous serpents, scorpions, &c.—shall seize, crush, and bite us, so that we shall certainly die. Let the calamities occasioned by fire, water, rulers, thieves,

BURMESE JUDGE, CLERKS, AND ATTENDANTS

and enemies oppress and destroy us, till we perish and come to utter destruction. Let us be subject to all the calamities that are within the body, and all that are without the body. May we be seized with madness, dumbness, blindness, deafness, leprosy, and hydrophobia. May we be struck with thunderbolts and lightning, and come to sudden death. In the midst of not speaking truth may I be taken with vomiting clotted black blood, and suddenly die before the assembled people. When I am going by water may the water nats assault me, the boat be upset, and the property lost; and may alligators, porpoises, sharks, and other sea monsters seize and crush me to death; and when I change worlds may I not arrive among men or nats, but suffer unmixed punishment and regret, in the utmost wretchedness, among the four states of punishment, Hell, Preta, Beasts, and Athurakai.'

'If I speak the truth, may I and my relations, through the influence of the ten laws of merit, and on account of the efficacy of truth, be freed from all calamities within and without the body, and may evils which have not yet come be warded far away. May the thunderbolts and lightning, the nat of the waters, and all sea animals love me, that I may be safe from them. May my prosperity increase like the rising sun and the waxing moon; and may the seven possessions, the seven laws, and the seven merits of the virtuous be permanent in my person; and when I change worlds may I not go to the four states of punishment, but attain the happiness of men and nats, and realise merit, reward, and perfect calm.'

The vernacular tongue of the Burmese has neither declension nor conjugation, and is very difficult for Europeans to learn. It is written from left to right, with no division between the words, and with letters most of which are circles or parts of circles. The

COPY OF AN OLD BURMESE PAINTING

alphabet contains forty-four letters. Printing is unknown. The Burmese write generally upon long pieces of black prepared paper, and with thick soapstone pencils. Knowledge is so widely diffused that there are few of the common people even who cannot read and write. Burmese literature consists for the most part of treatises upon theological and legal themes in the Pali dialect, and legends of the different Budhas, simple ballads, and books of astrology, cosmography, and astronomy in both the Pali and Burmese languages.

The religion of this nation is Budhism; and all the peoples of farther India profess the same faith. And Budhism is, without doubt, the most extensively diffused religion of the world—its followers numbering more than three hundred millions—though it has never been extended beyond the limits of Asia and its adjacent islands. The Burmese burn their dead, as do the Hindoos. The bodies of the priests are first embalmed, and then publicly burned with great demonstration.

Having seen all of interest in Rangoon, I determined to make an excursion up the great Irrawaddy river, as far as Mandalay, the capital of Ava, to pay my respects to His Majesty the King. One of a large flotilla of English steamers runs monthly to Bahmo, nearly a thousand miles from Rangoon, and there are weekly trips as far up as the capital. My English friend preferred to remain in Rangoon until my return. But nothing could change my plan, and so, all preparation being made, I embarked on the *flat* 'Pegu,' towed by the steamer 'Colonel Phayre,' on the 7th of April, for a long river voyage through British Burma, and into the very centre of the kingdom of Ava.

CHAPTER III.

UP THE IRRAWADDY

OWING to the shallow water we could not ascend the Rangoon river in order to enter the Irrawaddy, but were compelled to go by the Bassein Creek, and then through another called the China Bakeer, a narrow but deep stream, with low, jungle-clad banks. We had an excellent breeze during the day and through part of the night, until early morning, when so dense a fog enveloped us that the captain dropped anchor and awaited daylight, before effecting which, however, the vessels grounded near the bank, but managed after a while to work off the sandy bottom. At the breakfast table I noticed that the European passengers were eight in number, viz. three young ladies who were going to Thayet-myo, to see some relatives in the cantonments; a young married couple just out from England, who had taken passage to Mandalay—the gentleman was a mining engineer and under engagement with the King to prospect and bore for coal in

Ava—an assistant who accompanied him to the capital; and two English officers who were going to cantonments at Thayet-myo. Then, as 'upper deck' passengers, there was a company of English troops, and, as 'lower deck,' fully fifty Burmese, Chinese, Hindoos, and Mussulmans, who were 'booked' for various towns along the river. The natives pay Rs. 15 (a rupee is about 50 cts.) for passage to Mandalay, and provide their own food; the cabin passengers (European) pay Rs. 100, and Rs. 4 per diem additional for the table.

At noon on the second day from Rangoon we wheeled into the great Irrawaddy—the fourth river of the world in point of size, and the great highway into the dominions of his 'golden-footed' Majesty of Ava. The head of this celebrated river — styled 'Irrawaddy,' from the elephant of Indra—has not yet been actually discovered. It is probably, however, in the Himalaya mountains, east of Tibet, and near the Brahmapootra. This would make the entire river—which flows southerly and debouches into the Gulf of Martaban, or Bay of Bengal, through nine large mouths and a perfect labyrinth of small ones—about 1,400 miles in length. Its width varies from three to five miles when flowing through British Burma, and may, perhaps, average a mile or less from Mandalay to

Bhamo, a thousand miles from the sea. During a
great part of the year the channel is very intricate and
the current swift, but in May navigation is compa-
ratively easy, for in that month the river begins to
rise, and so continues until, during July, its height
above the lowest level will often be as much as forty
feet.

The scenery of the river became more interesting as
we proceeded. Sometimes for miles and miles we had
in sight nothing but the gigantic 'elephant' grass (so
called from its being, when in flourishing condition,
tall enough to conceal an elephant); then we would
have straggling villages—the huts made of bamboo
framework and palm mats, and covered with grass
roofs—and the people in gay-coloured garments would
flock to the river's bank, and squatting down upon
their haunches, gaze curiously at the wonderful fire-
boat and its 'barbarian' passengers; then followed a
long reach of sandy or muddy beach; then we would
pass miles of bananas, growing so rankly as to resemble the common jungle; and next a beautiful
fringe of the richest green foliage skirting the water's
edge. The first large village at which we stopped was
Myanoung. Some of us went on shore to see 'the
sights,' which consisted of half a dozen pagodas and

image-houses. I endeavoured to purchase a couple of small gilt images of Gaudama from a *pongyee* (priest), and offered a rupee in payment, but he either did not understand, or the offer was insufficient, or his religious scruples prevented the sale. The English authorities have built a brick market-house with an iron roof here for the accommodation and use of the natives. In it we saw an excellent variety of vegetables, fruits, and grains, also some few stalls containing dry goods. We had anchored near the bank, and, during the night, female coolies walked up and down the steep bluff, some fifty feet in height, carrying upon their heads large flat baskets of *paddy* (rice in the husk) on board the 'flat'—3,000 baskets of the grain being our cargo from that place.

Leaving Myanoung, we found the scenery improve still more. The high sand and mud banks which before had obstructed our view of the country inland now had disappeared, and we saw upon our left a low range of hills called the 'Arakan,' and upon our right plains covered with the densest of luxurious vegetation. The current became stronger, and the stream more tortuous, averaging in breadth less than a quarter of a mile. Near where a spur of the 'Arakan Hills' comes to an abrupt termination at the water's edge we ob

BURMESE IMAGE-HOUSE.

served a number of small niches cut in the face of the rock; there were forty in one row. These contained brick, and plaster, and marble (white marble of very good quality is quarried some forty or fifty miles from Ava) images of Gaudama, placed in various positions. One very large 'reclining' Gaudama especially claimed our attention. It must have been as

IRRAWADDY RIVER BOAT

much as thirty feet in length, and had been recently gilded and painted.

The curious river craft of various forms and size afforded us much amusement. Teak timber seemed to be the material most generally employed in their construction. They are of all lengths and widths, and the usual style is that modelled somewhat after the ancient Phœnician galleys. They have one lofty mast, and a long yard which supports an immense 'spread' of canvas; then there are usually two studding-sails and two upper sails; besides these are oars for eight, ten, or twelve rowers, when there is no wind; most of them have high and beautifully carved sterns, sitting on which the steersman directs the course of the vessel at will. The captain told me he had seen native boats whose yards were 110 feet in length, and whose ropes required 122 'blocks' (pulleys) to assist in the proper manœuvering of the sails. Against a strong current these boats sail but poorly; three or even four months from Rangoon to Mandalay, a distance of seven hundred miles, is the average time employed. The Burmese have also long narrow canoes, made from the single trunk of a tree, which they paddle very dextrously and swiftly. An upset, which, by the way, does not often happen, seems to occasion them no inconvenience; for should such an accident occur, they at once right their canoes, and swim round until they are partly baled, when they re-enter, and shaking themselves with a grin, paddle on as if nothing wet and uncomfortable had happened. The Irrawaddy boats and rafts are often the homes of large families. Their cargoes are usually salt fish, earth-oil (petroleum), *paddy*, and the condiment *ngapee*.

The Burmese men are remarkably indolent; the women, however, are industrious, but it is because the men compel them to do all the household work, at least the heaviest and most irksome part of it, and they will even sit about a place where their wives are at work, chatting and smoking, or else stretched upon the ground at full length asleep. If you give the native sufficient rice and *ngapee* to keep him just above the starving point, he will not work for Rs. 2 per diem; but take these articles of diet away, and he will cheerfully work for eight annas (25 cts.) However, like their neighbours the Chinese, they make excellent carpenters and blacksmiths. Marriage among the Burmese is a most peculiar institution, and the 'marriage knot' is very easily undone. If two persons are tired of each other's society, they dissolve partnership in the following simple and touching but conclusive manner: They respectively light two candles, and shutting up their hut, sit down and wait quietly until they are burned up. The one whose candle burns out first, gets up at once and leaves the house (and for ever), taking nothing but the clothes he or she may have on at the time; all else then becomes the property of the other party.

On the 12th we reached the large town of Prome. It lies upon a level plain, which juts out into the river a considerable distance. The hills round about were covered with custard apples, bananas, and many unknown plants. The fourth largest pagoda of Burma is situated in Prome; a party from the steamer, including myself, visited it. In general arrangements and character it resembles the Golden Pagoda at Rangoon; some of the images of Gaudama and some of the bells (cast from a mixed sort of metal resembling bronze) were of fair model and most extraordinary workmanship. The people evidently possess no small talent and ability for Easterns, but are too indolent to employ their faculties of mind or body in severer labour than eating, sleeping, chatting, and smoking. After our walk to the pagoda, which, situated upon a hill back of the town, is fully a hundred feet high, we visited several native huts, where the women were weaving, upon primitive looms, silk cloth of various gay patterns, stripes of alternate colours being the most esteemed. Between Prome and Thayet-myo the scenery of the river is most diversified; highlands and lowlands, islands and sandbanks, villages and boats, pagodas and temples, thick groves of palms near the banks and bare ranges of hills in the distance follow in quick succession and combine to make a picturesque scene, which is calculated long to remain green in the memory.

A day or two after leaving Thayet-myo we passed the steamer 'Nagpore' on her downward passage. The captain of this vessel reported 'all quiet at the capital,' though disturbances had been feared for some time previously, and for the following reason: It seems the King had built a very fine *tee*, or gilt umbrella, as a gift for the great *Shoay Dagon* pagoda at Rangoon, and wished to send it down in grand state with an escort of 10,000 troops. To this the British Commissioner objected, reducing the number of the escort to 300; but afterwards political and prudential motives had induced him to forbid any escort at all to accompany the *tee*. This decision naturally irritated the King exceedingly, and grave fears of rebellion or riot were entertained by the European residents at the capital.

The same day we passed the 'boundary pillars' which separate the British territory from that of the King of Ava, and anchored at a small village called Mengla for the night. As soon as we were made fast about thirty coolies, men and women, began to bring firewood on board. I was much surprised at the immense loads the women would carry—six or eight sticks of wood four feet long and nearly as large as one's leg—and these they carried from the top of the steep bank down to the steamer's deck, and threw into the hold.

CHAPTER IV.

PAGHAN AND THE OLD CAPITALS.

WHAT is generally known by the term Burma comprises two distinct regions: British or Lower Burma, which is under English rule, and Upper Burma, or more properly Ava, under the dominion of a native sovereign. British Burma embraces the three divisions of Arakan, on the eastern shores of the Bay of Bengal; Pegu, bordering on the Gulf of Martaban, on the south; and the long and narrow strip of country styled Tenasserim, which extends to the Isthmus of Kraw on the Malay peninsula. These divisions of the country are some of the results of two wars which the English Government have waged with Burma. The first, in 1824, caused by some insults offered to the British flag by the Viceroy of Rangoon, was settled two years later by ceding to the crown of England the provinces of Arakan and Tenasserim; the other, concluded in 1853, and brought about by native outrages towards European merchants and aggressions upon British territory, resulted in the annexation of the rich province of Pegu to the already enormously extended Anglo-Indian empire in the east. So that at the present day King Mounglon has no sea-board: Ava is entirely inland. The Irrawaddy river still remains as an outlet for the produce of the kingdom, though passing through foreign territory.

Proceeding up the river, we anchored on the 15th at the picturesque town of *Yaynan-gyoung*, with its long line of high-sterned fishing boats moored to the shore, and with scores of pagodas and temples crowning the neighbouring hill-tops for miles around. This town is noted for its export of earth-oil, or petroleum, so valuable to the Government as a source of revenue; the wells are situated about six miles distant from the river, and the oil is transported to this the nearest port in large earthen jars carried on carts drawn by bullocks, and then shipped to Rangoon. We received on board 3,000 baskets of *paddy* for the King at Mandalay, and the night was nearly spent before it was all shipped. The manner of loading was peculiar. Five large boats were rowed out from the shore in succession, and being made fast alongside, coolies carried the rice, in baskets holding sixty pounds each, upon their heads, and deposited it loose in the hold of our 'flat.'

The scenery was fast becoming dull and monotonous. The banks were of sand, and inland low and barren hills alone were to be seen. Pagodas and temples seemed to increase in number, and many *zyats* (free houses of rest for travellers) also appeared. The ruins of Paghan—a city founded over a thousand years ago—were an interesting study. No other signs of its former splendour now remain, however, than some pagodas and temples, a portion of very massive brick wall, and part of an old gateway. The ruins extend for eight miles along the bank of the river and two miles inland. The pagodas are of all sizes, shapes, and almost colours, and there are said to be nearly a thousand of them still standing. They are very massively built, the foundations being of stone and the superstructure of brick and plaster. Many of them are square structures raised over vaults, where Budhist priests dwell; then come several terraces gradually decreasing in width, and a bell-shaped spire, or in some of them a slender dome, rises above all. In the temples are many images of Gaudama, some of them of white alabaster and others of brick and plaster, painted red, and twenty feet in height.

The various forms and contents of the pagodas and temples now remaining render it extremely doubtful what people were formerly the builders or possessors of this ancient city of Paghan. Thus, besides the purely Budhistical monuments, there are statues bearing remarkable resemblances to those of the Egyptian Fetichism; others are of a Brahminical or Hindoo character; and some even, wonderful as it may seem, bespeak a Christian origin, or rather possess elements which have evidently been incorporated with the doctrines of Christianity. In support of this last statement I will quote the observations of a recent visitor at Paghan; says the author, speaking of one of the ruined buildings, 'On either side of the entrance to this pagoda, at the summit of the steps above the dragons, were two small figures of priests standing in long gowns, with umbrellas over their heads. One of these figures was the very counterpart of the statue of an English archbishop of the Middle Ages; and I was once before startled with a similar resemblance in a life-sized image of the same character, covered with gold mixed with black, near the foot of the staircase in the rooms of the Asiatic Society at Calcutta. Moreover, the umbrella over the little archbishop bore a remarkable similarity to the small circular roof over the pulpit of an English cathedral, which is popularly supposed to serve as a sounding board. Other resemblances, including the ground plan of most of the temples, which is shaped like a cross after the manner of European cathedrals, have induced some missionaries to presume that these buildings have a Christian origin. This idea seems somewhat preposterous. It is far more likely that there is a Budhist element in the Christianity of the dark ages, of which monasticism evidently forms a part, just in the same way that there is a great deal of Platonism in the early Fathers.'

Just after leaving Paghan the bank rises in a high sandstone bluff, and cut in the almost inaccessible face of this were many small openings which led to equally small chambers within, where some ascetic priests had taken up their abode. The next town we reached was called Tsagaing. It lies at the foot of some beautiful hills which are almost covered with pagodas, temples, griffins, and long, winding staircases. Some of the stone staircases, leading from the little town to the pagodas on the tops of the hills, were as much as half a mile in length. Before reaching Ava we noticed on the left bank of the river an immense bell-shaped pagoda. It was built after the Mussulman model found in India, and reminded me strongly of some of the tombs which are to be seen in the old cities near Delhi. This pagoda is esteemed very holy, and once a year a great *mala*, or religious festival of different nations, is held in its honour. Ava, formerly the capital, and built on an island, is now only a miserable village, though the massive ruins still standing attest its former splendour. The ancient city wall, sixteen feet high and ten feet thick, formerly enclosed six or seven miles of buildings. Ava was very famous for its silk manufacture in olden times. Amarapoora, which was also at one time the metropolis of Burma, and contained 175,000 inhabitants, was but dimly seen on the left bank of the river, six miles east of Ava.

The Burmese have been accustomed to change their capital rather frequently for many years back; this was owing, sometimes, to revolution; again to royal caprice, or superstition, or else change of dynasty. Thus Ava was first made capital A.D. 1364; next Monchobo (about 1740) was used as the seat of government by King Alompra (surnamed 'the Great,' though a man of low birth, who having first driven the Talains out of Pegu, caused himself to be proclaimed king, then built a palace at Dagong, changing its name to Rangoon, made a treaty with the English, and established a new dynasty —that at present on the throne), it being his native town; then, in 1782, the court was removed to Amarapoora; in 1819 the government was changed back to

Ava, the reigning king being thus advised by the court astrologers. In 1839 Ava was destroyed by an earthquake, and then again Monchobo became the capital; not long afterwards Amarapoora was a second time chosen as the residence of the fickle court; next again, for the third time, Ava, and now, since 1857, Mandalay has been the abode of royalty and power.

Mandalay is but a few miles above Amarapoora, on the same bank of the river. On the 18th we anchored at the port or landing of the 'golden city,' and so safely reached the proposed limit of my excursion north from Rangoon.

CHAPTER V.

MANDALAY

ALL that can be seen of the city of Mandalay from the river is a confused mixture of spires, and towers, and temple-tops appearing above the rich masses of foliage with which it is thickly surrounded. We anchored at twelve o'clock by the side of a dreary sandbank, with some fine large trees a little distance inland, a few bamboo huts in sight, and the usual complement of dirty and curious natives squatting along the bank—the landing being three miles distant from the city. Just behind us in the river lay a large steamer belonging to the King, but which was not then in use. His Majesty owns several others which are in the same predicament; and, besides, he is building ten steamers of a larger size and better constructed— for what purpose I did not learn. These steamers lie upon the stocks in rows, and are covered with huge sheds; they are being built of solid teak timber, and the work is done by the natives under the direction of

VIEW OF THE CITY OF MANDALAY.

a European, who bears the proud title of Shipwright to H.M. the King of Ava.

On the opposite side of the river, and four or five miles from Mandalay, there is a very large bell, the largest in the world with the exception of that at Moscow. It is said to be twelve feet high, and more than sixteen feet in diameter at the lip, and could easily contain twenty people. There is no clapper, as in former times it was beaten from without. It emits no sound now. It is still slung from a great beam by a huge copper hook or sling; but the hook has given way, and the bell now rests upon some blocks of wood carved in strange, grotesque figures. The thickness of the metal of the bell varies from six inches to twelve, and its actual weight is about *ninety tons*. The exterior measurements of this bell do not much exceed those of ' the great bell of Pekin,' that being thirteen feet in diameter and fourteen feet in height, but weighing only fifty-three and one-half tons, being much thinner than the Burman bell. Early on the morning following our arrival Mr. Seng-Ko, a Chinese gentleman to whom I had brought a letter of introduction, called on board. I was much surprised at the abilities of this gentleman. He is one of the richest men at Mandalay, speaks English fluently, and enjoys the especial confidence and friendship of the King, having a private *entrée* to 'the Presence' by day or night. He remained to breakfast, and before leaving promised 'to do his best' to obtain me an audience with His Majesty.

At six o'clock the next morning Mr. Seng-Ko's servant arrived with a pony; he also brought a note from his master, which read: 'I have seen His Majesty personally, and spoken to him about your desire to see him. H.M. is happy, and has desired me to bring you up to-day (Thursday). I send you the pony; the boy will be your guide to—Yours faithfully,' &c. I did not delay for my breakfast, but mounting the beautiful little Pegu pony, started at once for the city. Riding up the sandbank, which is covered by the river in the wet season, a little inland we passed, first, a large new palace, which the King has just built as a residence during the warmest months of the year. It consists of an immense square of fantastic-shaped buildings, with pretty little carved and peaked roofs, the whole lavishly ornamented with fancy wood carvings. A bamboo fence, twenty feet high, and fully a quarter of a mile square, surrounds the royal mansion. Then we crossed an immense plain and saw before us the numerous pagoda and temple spires of 'the golden city,' and beyond a small eminence called 'Mandalay

Hill,' covered with monasteries and bell towers. During a great part of the year this plain is inundated with water, and then for locomotion the natives are compelled to betake themselves to canoes and rafts *in lieu* of ponies and bullock-carts. Mandalay is a *new* city; as recently as 1855 the area now thickly peopled was merely farm land; building began the following year, and the Court have resided there since 1857. The houses in the suburbs of Mandalay do not at all differ from those in any of the villages seen along the river; they are simple, frail structures of bamboo framework and mat covering, with grass or palm-leaf thatched roofs, and are raised some four or five feet from the ground upon wooden piles, as a precaution against inundations, dampness, fevers, and dysentery. This lower story is sometimes used as a stable for the domestic animals.

In the principal streets of the suburbs the majority of the houses are either built of brick or large bricks are *nailed* to the timbers and sidings, and then the whole exterior is thickly plastered with lime or mud. Some of the Chinese shops are two stories in height; these present a very neat and tidy appearance. Numbers of pagodas and temples and *kyoungs* (schools or monasteries) were seen in all directions. As many of the houses are built of very inflammable material, and are crowded so closely together, and as the natives are so apathetic and phlegmatic, a fire becomes a terrible scourge. One occurred several weeks before my visit, and destroyed about five thousand houses; our road led through the burned district, and the desolate picture there presented was fearful to behold. The ground was covered with the charred and blackened remnants of huts and household goods, the dead trees were heaped about and still smoking, and, as if to heighten the mournful spectacle, here and there, at considerable intervals, might be seen little mat hovels which had just been erected by some of the sufferers, who had saved only enough to shelter themselves from the scorching mid-day sun.

At last we halted before a plain brick house built much in the European style; and, dismounting, I was cordially welcomed by the Chinaman, who, after he had examined my present for the King—a large magnifying glass, with a bright gilt rim and an ivory handle—and pronounced it both novel and appropriate, ordered his own pony to be brought, and then we rode at once to the palace—distant about a mile and a half from his residence. By the wayside I noticed a large image of Gaudama (the last Budha), which had its head protected from the sun by a broad-brimmed and peaked-crowned Chinese hat; the picture produced by the smiling, gilt-faced god shaded by such a curious head-gear was most ludicrous.

There are several Asiatic nations represented in Mandalay, the population of which is about a hundred thousand, but the Chinese, dwelling mostly in the suburbs and southern parts of the city, have the greater part of the trade in their hands; the Europeans, living in the western quarter, all told, number but fourteen, some of them being officials of the English Government and a few being engaged in trade.

The city proper is a square—a mile on each side—and is surrounded by a lofty and very thick wall of loose brick (unplastered) with a notched parapet, and having a broad and deep moat filled with clear water. There are three gates on each side, and macadamised streets about a hundred feet in width, leading from them, intersect the city at right angles; then between these there are small and irregular streets and by-paths. Along the sides of the larger avenues there run channels for carrying water (which is brought from the river in a canal fifteen miles long) throughout the city. Each gateway is surmounted by a lofty pyramidal-shaped wooden tower with the customary terraced roof, and at irregular intervals there are turrets raised a little higher than the wall and surmounted by small wooden pavilions of the same model as those over the great gates. We crossed the moat on a massive wooden bridge, and passed through one of the western gateways—the only one through which corpses are allowed to be taken from the city, as my guide observed. The gates are of enormous height and thickness, and are built of teak beams fastened together with huge iron bolts. A few half-naked soldiers, who were stationed as a guard just within the entrance, saluted us by squatting on the ground in true native fashion. On reaching the palace we left our ponies and proceeded on foot, entering through the south gate.

The outer palace walls are double, the one being thirty feet distant from the other; both are built of brick, and enclose about seventy-two acres of ground. The western gate is strictly set apart for the use of the ladies of the Court; near the one at which we entered were some barracks and a guard-house, before which latter, standing in a row, were five of the King's soldiers. They wore brass hats, shaped somewhat like a broad-brimmed 'panama,' with griffins in front; red coats, with green facings (British army pattern); their legs and feet were bare; and their only weapon consisted of

THE PALACE, MANDALAY

an immense *dah*, an instrument shaped precisely like our butchers' cleavers, and which they held over their shoulders in a most laughable serio-comic manner. It is not always, indeed, that the Burmese soldiers adopt even so much uniform as this; their profession can often only be known by a tattooed mark on the back of the neck. Walking into the square, which was filled with natives of all ranks passing in every direction, I saw upon the right a small pagoda, farther on a bell tower, and in the left-hand corner a magazine and some buildings filled with light ordnance; next came the 'High Court,' and then the 'Royal Mint,' while towering high above all rose the graceful spire of the magnificent 'Hall of Audience.'

In a small building, or rather shed (for it was a very plain bamboo affair, and contained no furniture, carpets, or vessels of any kind), near the High Court-house, was the *Pakhan Mengyee*, or Foreign Minister, and upon him we made our first call. The shed was entirely open on the front side, and there a low bamboo platform was placed; and upon this we sat, and taking off our shoes and leaving them underneath (agreeably to Burmese etiquette) we walked in a rather humble manner into the diplomatic office and sat, or more properly lay, down upon the floor on our hips, with the feet thrust far to the rear, for the soles of the feet must never be shown when in the presence of a superior. The *Pakhan Mengyee* was taking his breakfast, but he at once entered into conversation with my Chinese *cicerone* concerning my nationality, age, business, travels, &c. This gentleman, whose rank is only second to members of the royal family, appeared to be upwards of sixty years of age; he had a rather sinister and crafty countenance and a very pompous and conceited manner. The minister was plainly dressed, with his hair 'put up' in a knot and a white handkerchief twisted into a coil and bound once round his head, the two ends left out and appearing just above the hair, like the war plumes of a North American Indian. I afterwards noticed that all the Government officials and clerks wore this style of turban or head-dress, instead of the usually seen vari-coloured bandanna.

Leaving the Foreign Office, we passed round the *Hlot-daw*, or 'High Court'—a large but not imposing building, painted red, with gilt ornamental work; and in which the four principal *Woongyees*, or ministers of the King, sit to adjudicate all appeal cases—and were about to enter, through a double line of walls, the enclosure which contains the palace buildings, when our attention was attracted by a regiment of native Burmese soldiers, who had been out at target practice. They marched by us in column, four deep, clothed in nothing but the *doty* (waist cloth), and carrying huge old-fashioned muskets, closely resembling the historic blunderbuss of the sixteenth century. Judging from the appearance of these troops I should say that a thoroughly equipped European soldier would be a match for at least ten of them, and yet it has been said that the Burman soldier fights well under favouring circumstances. But the chief excellence of a Burman army lies in the absence of the *impedimenta*; the soldier carries his bed (a mat or blanket) at one end of his matchlock, a package of powder and a brass kettle at the other, and his provisions (rice, salt, and the half-putrid fish condiment called *ngapee*) in a cloth about his waist. After a few words with the 'Captain of the Guard,' who showed me some 'Schneider' rifles recently imported, we entered the square which contains the temporal abode of the 'Lord of Earth and Air.' Near the centre of this enclosure is the imposing 'Hall of Audience,' which is only used on great or solemn occasions, as for the reception of foreign ambassadors or the celebration of royal *fêtes*. The building consists of a lofty tower, with terraces of little roofs rising one above the other, and crowned by the gold umbrella in the centre, and two smaller ones on each wing, over a long central court or hall (both also in the many-roofed style of Burmese architecture), and the whole gaudily painted in red and gold and covered with ornate carvings and decorations of brass, china, and glass. In front of the grand staircase are two immense cannon, mounted on primitive carriages having solid wooden 'block' wheels. On the right hand were barracks, a carriage foundry, and the royal gardens; while on the left were ordnance stores, the abode of the 'white elephant,' a building filled with canoes, and some sheds containing war and work elephants — these latter black.

We then called at the office of the Prime Minister, whom we found, with his assistant, discussing a wholesome breakfast. The food for each was brought by servants in four or five little bowls placed upon trays, and they ate with their fingers, taking something from each bowl in turn. The meal embraced vegetables and fish, rice, *ngapee*, greens, and spices; water only, from wooden cups, was drunk during the breakfast. My Chinese friend here learned that the King had just terminated his first 'audience,' and so I would have to wait nearly two hours, and then attend the second. During this time he introduced me to some other of

the Government officials, with all of whom he seemed
to be on most excellent terms. The conversation with
all of them was similar to that held with the Foreign
Minister, except one with the *Yaw-Ahtween-Woon*, or
Minister of the Interior, who was singularly and not
altogether politely curious, asking such embarrassing
questions as how much money I expended in travelling,
what business my father did, what I was travelling for,
and why I did not settle down somewhere. His Excellency imagined I must be travelling for political
purposes, and could not comprehend any other motive
for visiting foreign countries. He was a middle-aged
man, a thorough politician of the unscrupulous sort,
and I doubt not exceedingly cunning; but yet it
appears he had quite recently been forbidden by the
King to transact any further business with Europeans,
owing to some discrepancies in the official returns, and
his duties and powers had been transferred for the
time to one of the royal secretaries. Near the office
of the Minister of the Interior I saw a half-dozen men
who were shackled with their hands behind them, and
exposed, bare-headed, to the noon-day rays of the sun;
they were prisoners for debt, and would be held in
'durance vile' until some friend advanced sufficient
funds to satisfy the just claims of their creditors.

At the *Yaw-Ahtween-Woon's* office I met a very intelligent young Burman, who had studied in Paris, spoke French fluently and English fairly; his Burmese title being *Pangyet Woon*, or 'Governor of the Glass Manufactories'—a rather irrelevant appellation, for there are no such manufactories in Ava. I conversed with him nearly an hour, and obtained much valuable information concerning his country and countrymen and women. In a small pamphlet published in Rangoon (November 1870) I found the following account of this talented native gentleman, which presents a notable, though not unique, example of the capabilities and intelligence of the higher class of Burmese youth— the nobles: 'At eighteen years of age he was sent by the late Crown Prince to Calcutta, to be educated in English at Doreton College. After four years' residence at Calcutta this young Burmese gentleman returned to Mandalay, and during the voyage he made the acquaintance of Count de Lacy, who was a passenger on board the steamer, and could speak English. After staying a few months at Mandalay the King was induced by his French proclivities to send the young Burman to Paris, in charge of the Count, to study French. After acquiring the language he studied sciences for five years at the institution known as the

Pantheon, and here he took the degrees of both Bachelor and Master of Arts. Finally he studied for three years at the Central Imperial School of Arts and Manufactures, and obtained a diploma. His career in Europe was brought to a close by the rebellion in 1866, in which the Crown Prince was slain, and early in 1867 he was recalled to Mandalay by the King.' In addition to his duties as one of the royal secretaries, he had been appointed to sit with the Political Agent (English) as judge of the mixed court at Mandalay. Well, indeed, would it be for King Mounglon were there more such as he at the Court of Ava!

In one of the offices, a minor court, there seemed to be a great deal of business transacted, for there were as many as thirty or forty people waiting all the time; each seemed to speedily finish his errand, whatever it might have been, but more coming in kept the room continually full. In asking favours of an official the natives prostrate themselves upon their stomachs, clasp the hands as if in the act of worship, and scarcely dare to raise their eyes from the floor. The Government clerks 'keep' their accounts, as is usual throughout Burma, upon long strips of a prepared black paper, which is very rough; it is written upon with slate pencils or sticks of French chalk the size of one's finger. After remaining in the Court-room about twenty minutes an officer came with a message that the King was ready to give 'audience,' and so, preceded by two of the grand ministers, we approached the Mhaw-gaw—the Crystal Palace—passing through still another gate in a low brick wall. A huge elephant looked calmly at us from a red shed near the road, but we did not stop; and soon after, leaving our shoes at the foot, mounted a long flight of stone stairs and entered another office, where our arrival was announced to His Majesty. While awaiting an answer I strolled into the 'Hall of Audience' to see the throne. It is a flat, raised *dais*, perhaps eight feet square, richly gilded, and on either side are the white and gold silk umbrellas, symbols of royalty (it is said that umbrellas were a sign of rank in ancient Nineveh, and they are so esteemed by most Asiatic nations at the present day). The hall is gaily painted, and the ceiling is supported by enormous round teak pillars. Banquets, at which the table service is of pure gold and silver, are sometimes served here. In the rear of this building, and connected with it, are the minor audience chambers, one or the other being used at the humour of the King, and each being named from their peculiar style of decoration; thus there is the 'Golden Palace,' which is entirely covered with gold (?), and the Mhaw-gaw, or 'Crystal Palace' (already mentioned), and so called because it is adorned with trimmings in isinglass, porcelain, and glass—small mirrors.

CHAPTER VI.

AUDIENCE WITH THE KING OF AVA.

AFTER waiting five or ten minutes we were summoned to a small pillared portico, open on two sides. At our backs there was a golden door leading to another chamber, and before us was a large green baize curtain, extending from the ceiling to the floor of another room which was some few feet above us. In the centre of this screen was an opening about ten feet square; here a red velvet cushion and a pair of silver-mounted *binoculars* were laid upon the floor, where there was an elegantly carpeted staircase connecting the two chambers. The roof was supported by immense pillars, grouped around the bases of two of which were the royal umbrellas and other *insignia*. No one save the King is allowed to possess a *white* umbrella, and princes of the blood are allowed to have *two* umbrellas (gilt, with poles ten or fifteen feet in length attached) carried above them by their servants when they walk or ride in public—ministers but *one*. There were about half a dozen princes in the 'Audience Chamber,' among them the heir-apparent, an intelligent as well as handsome young man, plainly dressed, *excepting* a pair of immense cluster diamond ear-rings. Our party —for there were several others whom we found waiting—was disposed in the following order: The princes sat upon the right, then came the *Yaw-Ahtween-Woon*, then another minister, then myself, next Mr. Seng-Ko, then two ex-ministers of the former King; adjoining them were two Portuguese Roman Catholic missionaries, and then two commercial gentlemen upon the extreme left; besides these, in the rear, were some dozen or more clerks, who were paying their respects to His Majesty upon the receipt of new appointments, each offering a large basket of fruit in support of his loyal feelings. Our presents were displayed before us, placed on little wooden stands about a foot in height. The natives were all prostrating themselves flat upon their stomachs, with their noses nearly touching the carpets and their eyes cast down in a most abject and servile manner.

In a few moments we heard two or three muffled booms—taps on a large tom-tom probably—and then all of us becoming at once silent, the King appeared, and quietly and slowly laid himself down, reclining against the velvet cushion and only partially facing the audience. At the same time one of the queens entered and placed a golden spittoon, betel-box, *chatty* (with water), and cup on the floor before him. The King is a short, stout, pleasant, though, like many of his ministers, an exceeding crafty-looking gentleman, fifty-four years of age. His hair was thin and was tied in the usual Burmese knot; the head was high at the crown, showing 'self-esteem,' large, and the eyes were closely set, indicating cunning (if we are to believe phrenology and physiognomy); the neck was thick, expressive of vitality and physical power, and the face close shaven, excepting a thin black moustache. His dress was very plain and simple, consisting merely of a white *engie*, a white linen jacket, and a silk *putso*, a cloth worn around the hips and thighs; there were no ornaments in the ears, though their lobes contained holes nearly an inch in diameter, which did not improve the expression of his countenance very materially. His Majesty first took up his opera glass, though we were not more than twenty feet distant, and surveyed us in a very grave and leisurely manner, ending with a flourish of the glass, as if to say, 'Now, then, for business.' The royal secretary read aloud our names, business, and the list of the presents which were placed before us; this was done in a loud, drawling style, and concluded with a sort of supplicating moan.

His Majesty then began the conversation through the Minister and my Chinese friend as interpreters. After the usual questions concerning my age, business, residence, and travels, the King said he wished me to convey to my Government the sentiment that 'he had a great partiality for Americans, and wished them to come over and colonise in his dominions.' But a word preliminary: it seems that I had the honour to be the first *American* presented at the Court of Ava (excepting a mechanical engineer, who was in His Majesty's *employ* ten or twelve years ago), and that the King in his astuteness graciously thought me a *spy*, or at least that I was visiting Burma for political purposes, and consequently had some influence with as well as instructions from the Government at home. It was in vain that I protested being a simple traveller, visiting different countries for the purpose of studying their geography, climate, productions; the people—their manners and customs, government, religion, laws, language, literature, industries, and commerce—and all for the improvement of mind and health of body, and that I had travelled about twelve thousand miles more especially to pay my respects to the King of Ava, and to see the wonderful white elephant, about which I had heard and read so much in my own country; but to no purpose, for it was quite evident His Majesty thought politics were surely my main object and end. Promising to make his wishes known to the proper authorities at home did not seem to be alone sufficient for his purposes, for he said he would keep me in Mandalay while I wrote, and until an answer came from America. At this I demurred of course, when His Majesty said if I would remain he would give me a house, living, and *as many Burmese wives as I wished* (a rather tempting offer, for the women of the upper classes are both pretty and modest), and, furthermore, he would 'make my fortune.' I was fast becoming very much interested, and slightly excited as well. His Majesty wished to make also a commercial treaty with America, and my services would be indispensable. Thus were alluring nets spread for my feet and enticing temptations presented to me. Still I was not then prepared to enter the King's service; the idea was too new and novel, the change—from republican America and steam ploughs to monarchical Burma and white elephants—too great. 'I must have time to consider His Majesty's gracious offers,' said I to the interpreter. 'You will never have a better chance,' was returned from the King. Seeing me still reluctant, the King condescendingly offered to 'make me a great man'—to give me high rank among his own nobles and princes. To this I answered my duty was first to my parents, and next to my own country, and that I would return to the latter and consult with the former, and then, *if they were willing*, I would be most happy to accept his magnificent and unusually gracious terms. He replied, 'It might then be too late;' and there the matter dropped, and the conversation was changed to other topics, though the King was evidently not a little vexed at my obstinacy, and doubtless thought me mad or certainly very foolish not to accept such generous proposals. One of the missionaries then presented some petitions, which were referred to the proper minister; some State business was transacted; a present of Rs. 100 was brought me ('to use for my travelling expenses or to purchase a memento of my presentation at the Court of "His Golden-Footed Majesty"'), and then the audience was terminated by the King suddenly rising and abruptly retiring from the room.

One of his queens or concubines (he has four of the former and about a hundred of the latter) who, though out of sight, had been fanning the King with a gorgeous fan of peacock's feathers during the audience, now took a peep at us, of course exhibiting herself at the same time, and such a beautiful creature I have rarely looked upon before and perchance never shall see again. She was one of the veritable 'houris of Paradise,' an oriental pearl of indescribable loveliness and symmetry. I will not attempt a description; but the King's liberal offers came at once to mind, and I felt what a great sacrifice it would be to return to my native land, and refuse—nay, almost spurn—rank, wealth, and beauty under the peacock banner and golden umbrella of His Majesty of Ava.

The 'audience' lasted over an hour. The King seemed to have very respectable ideas of America and a high appreciation of the (usually conceded) enterprise and industry of her people; perhaps he wished Americans to settle in Burma as a sort of political offset to the English, whose power—now owning two-thirds of ancient Burma—is naturally very great, but I think his main idea was simply to obtain from the United States a commercial treaty advantageous to himself. His Majesty's use of the binoculars, which he invariably employs in *all* audiences, is not altogether pleasant; but the manner in which he would scan our countenances while replying to some of his *commanding* speeches was most amusing. His voice is soft and low, and he speaks in a very deliberate manner, taking ample time to arrange his thoughts before giving them utterance.

The present King is a son of the famous Tharawaddi; his brother—the eldest legitimate son—assumed the government in 1845, but, proving a tyrant, was deposed and succeeded by King Mounglon in 1853. In 1857 he removed the capital from Amarapoora to Mandalay. The King, little thinking that he would ever attain the crown, had in early youth taken the vows of a *phongyee*, or Budhist priest, and lived secluded in a monastery until his accession. Like his predecessors his reign has not been without its troubles. In 1866 a rebellion broke out headed by two of the King's sons, the Mengon and Mengondyne princes, having for its object the dethronement of their father. The attempt failed, and the former is a refugee in the Shan States, while the latter resides under British protection in Bengal. As regards the events of the King's rule much might be said of blame and something also of praise. The Government is a despotism; among many others we notice the royal title of 'Lord of the Power of Life and Death.' The *Holt-daw* (Council of State), composed of the four principal ministers of

State, are the executive officers of the Government; they also try all appeal cases, forming a high court for that purpose, and receiving ten per cent. of the property in suit, are said to derive very handsome incomes from this source alone. The tyranny and weight of the King's rule is most felt at, or in the immediate vicinity of, the capital, the remote districts being almost independent, and paying but little more heed to the ruling monarch than to swear allegiance whenever visited by his officers. And so limited in extent of territory is the real power of the King that the people dwelling upon the borders of Yunan are said to acknowledge the sovereignty of the local rulers of the Emperor of China as well as those of the King of Ava, and so enjoy privileges from both Governments. At present there is a royal monopoly of the *paddy* (rice) and cotton and other leading products—marble, amber, gold, copper, coal, and guns above a certain size (all over Rs. 100 in value). The King dare not leave his palace for fear of foul play, and he has consequently never seen his own war canoes or steamers, nor has he ever visited his new palace built near the river.

The Government is 'rotten to the very core;' bribery and corruption reign paramount. The King appropriates most of the revenue; many of his ministers receive no salary at all; and the King buys goods of merchants and serves them out as pay to his troops and followers, who afterwards have to sell them in the bazaars at half-price; besides, the country bitterly suffers ' from the extortionate duties, from the grinding taxation, and from the cruelties and oppressions that daily transpire (boys of tender years and infirm old men being flogged to death in the streets, or publicly crucified with a barbarity that beggars description), and from the guild of brokers, who rule the markets according to the orders of the King or his ministers, so that no one can buy or sell save through these brokers. And yet the King has shown some appreciation of the advantages of western civilisation. He offers good inducements to European mechanics and engineers to establish themselves in Mandalay. His Majesty has succeeded in bringing his country into telegraphic communication with India and Europe. The introduction of the electric telegraph into Burma is thus curiously described by my friend the *Yaw-Ahtween-Woon* (Minister of the Interior): 'The present founder of the city of Mandalay or Rutuapon, Builder of the Royal Palace, Ruler of the Sea and Land, Lord of the Celestial Elephant and Master of many White Elephants, Owner of the

Shekyah or Indra's Weapon, Lord of the Power of Life and Death, and Great Chief of Righteousness, being exceedingly anxious for the welfare of his people, in the year 1231 introduced the telegraph, a science the elements of which may be compared to thunder and lightning for rapidity and brilliancy, and such as his royal ancestors in successive generations had never attempted.' Orientals are profuse in high-sounding and adulatory diction; the foregoing article does not contain the half of the titles pertaining to King Mounglon.

CHAPTER VII.

THE WHITE ELEPHANT.

HAVING put on our shoes at the bottom of the palace staircase, we went to see the so-called white elephant. One of the proudest titles of the King of Ava is 'Lord of the White Elephant,' though the King of Siam at Bangkok is also the possessor of one or more of these sacred beasts. The Mandalay animal I found to be a male of medium size, with *white eyes* and a forehead and ears *spotted* white, appearing as if they had been rubbed with pumice-stone or sand-paper, but the remainder of the body was as 'black as coal.' He was a vicious brute, chained by the fore-legs in the centre of a large shed, and was surrounded with the 'adjuncts of royalty'—gold and white cloth umbrellas, an embroidered canopy above, and some bundles of spears in the corners of the room. The attendants told me that a young one, captured in the north-eastern part of British Burma, near Tounghoo, had recently died, after a short residence in the capital, and that the king had been 'out of sorts' ever since. This animal was suckled by twelve women, hired for the express purpose; these elephant 'wet-nurses' receiving Rs. 50 per mensem, and thinking it a great honour to serve in such capacity.

The white elephant, well named the Apis of the Budhists, has long been an appendage to Burman state. Mr. Ralph Fitch, who travelled through Burma about the year 1582, speaking of the king who reigned at that time, says, in his quaint, black-letter folio, that "among the rest he hath foure white elephants, which are very strange and rare, for there is none other king that hath them but he; if any other king hath one, hee will send vnto him for it. When any of these white elephants is brought vnto the king, all the merchants in the city are commanded to see them and to giue him a present of halfe a ducat, which doth come to a great summe, for that there are many merchants in the city. After that you have given your present, you may come and see them at your pleasure, although they stand in the king's house. The king, in his title, is called the king of the white elephants. If any other king haue one, and will not send it him, he will make warre with him for it, for he had rather lose a great part of his kingdome than not to conquere him. They do very great seruice vnto these white elephants; euery one of them standeth in a house gilded with golde, and they doe feede in vessels of siluer and gilt. One of them, when he doth go to the riuer to be washed, as euery day they do, goeth under a canopy of clothe, of golde or of silke, carried ouer him by sixe or eight men, and eight or ten men goe before him, playing on drummes, shawmes (clarionets), or other instruments; and when he is washed, and cometh out of the riuer, there is a gentleman which doth wash his feet in a siluer basin, which is his office giuen him by the king. There is no account made of any blacke elephant, be he neuer so great. And surely there be woonderful faire and great, and some be nine cubites in height." Again, in Father Sangermano's 'Description of the Burmese Empire,' some two hundred years later, we have interesting accounts of the capture, transportation (to the capital), and more than royal treatment of the white elephant: how, when caught in the forests of Pegu, it was bound with scarlet cords and waited upon by the highest mandarins of the empire; how the place where it was taken being infested with mosquitoes, a silken net was made to protect it from them; how it was transported to Amarapoora in a boat having a pavilion draped with gold-embroidered silk, and covered with a roof similar to those covering the royal palaces; how, on its arrival in the city, a grand festival, continuing for three days, was celebrated in its honour; and how the most costly presents were brought to it by the mandarins, one offering a vase of gold weighing 480 ounces. This animal was honoured no less at its demise than during life. Being a female, its funeral was conducted with the same forms and rites as those practised at the death of a queen. The body was burned upon a pile of sassafras, sandal, and other aromatic woods, the pyre being fired with the aid of four immense gilt bellows placed at its corners. Three days afterwards its ashes were gathered by the chief mandarins, enshrined in gilt urns, and buried in the royal cemetery. A superb mausoleum, of a pyramidal shape, built of brick, richly painted and gilt, was subsequently raised over the tomb. If this elephant had been a male, it would have been interred with the same ceremonial as that used for the sovereign. And even at this day the 'celestial' white elephants are still the objects of great veneration, royal favour, and attention; aside from their divine character of (being) trans-

migrating Budhas, their possession, according to
Burmese superstition, is considered to bring prosperity
to the country in peace and good fortune in war, and
therefore their death is regarded as nothing less than
a national calamity. At such times the entire nation
shave their heads, and perform such deeds of sorrow
and mourning as are customary on the loss of the
nearest and dearest of their relatives.

In one shed were some large gilded war-boats, and
in another were the royal palanquins and carriages, all
richly gilded, the former of fantastic and whimsical
model, and the latter of English design, if not manufacture. The 'Royal Gardens' we did not visit. They
are said to be laid out in squares, crossed in different
places by canals of brickwork, in which the water is
seven fathoms in depth. The pathways run in every
direction, and grottoes are thickly interspersed among
them. We inspected the artillery sheds, and observed
that most of the cannon were of small calibre and
antique manufacture; some of them were as much as
twenty feet in length and scarcely more than four inches
bore from muzzle to vent; they had been captured
from the Siamese. We next visited the 'Royal
Herald's' office, and obtained a permit to take the
present with which His Majesty had honoured me

through the palace gates. This 'pass' was simply a piece of prepared palm-leaf about five inches in length and a little more than one in width; the order was an engraved *intaglio* (in ordinary Burmese circular character), and in one corner was the King's Treasury stamp impressed on *basso relievo*. Strips of palm-leaf are also used by scholars. They usually write or engrave with a sharp iron instrument (a style) upon pieces about two feet long and two and a half inches broad, and with a number of these strips and two thin boards of the same size for covers they form their books.

Having gained the street beyond the outermost wall, we remounted our ponies and rode to Mr. Seng-Ko's house. My host's pretty little Burmese wife then 'served up' a very palatable *tiffin* (lunch), and over our cheroots and tea we discussed the events of the morning, the future of Burma, the present state of China, and the rapid rise and prospects of the Chinese population of San Francisco and California. Speaking of *tea*, this valuable commodity is raised, in small quantity, upon the northern hills, those bordering upon the province of Yunan, in China; but the Burmese devote the leaf to a far different purpose from that employed by the surrounding nations and by ourselves. Instead of steeping the leaves and drinking the warm and refreshing decoction obtained therefrom, they make a sort of salad of them, together with garlic, adding some kind of oil and condiment.

About three o'clock in the afternoon my obliging Chinese friend accompanied me on a walk through the bazaars and market, and to see the King's war canoes. The bazaars were similar to those of Rangoon for variety and quality of goods, containing chiefly Chinese silks and British cloths, Bengal steel goods, checkered bandannas, *putsoes* (cloths worn round the hips), earthenware, porcelain, amber—sold for Rs. 2 per pound in the capital—carved marble and wooden images of Gaudama, paper umbrellas and copper from China, &c. Here I obtained a complete collection of Burmese coins—made of copper, lead, pewter, silver, and gold. The silver coins have a copper alloy of about fifteen per cent. Interest is very high—sixty per cent. per annum being sometimes charged. Much of the trade is carried on by means of barter, petroleum being the chief circulating medium; rice also is used as a money exchange in some parts of the country. The prices demanded seemed moderate, though a European is always, and perhaps justly, asked to pay more than a native. We saw some cotton goods of English manufacture and importation, which were sold cheaper even than the products of the domestic looms. The market was very large, and contained good varieties of vegetables and fish, but no meats. It consisted of about a hundred little bamboo sheds, built together, and the different articles were arranged in sections. It was a long walk to the war canoes, and made under a burning sun—therm. 112° (Fah.) in the shade—but I felt amply repaid on beholding the curious navy belonging to the King. These canoes lie in a small creek which runs from the river up to the city. They are very long, with both prow and stern curling up high, and are paddled by forty men usually, sometimes sixty; most of the boats are handsomely gilded on the outside and painted red within. A very fine barge, with decks and apartments, Mr. Seng-Ko pointed out as being used exclusively by the queens; it is drawn or towed by war boats. The King's barge is the grandest of them all, but being too distant to observe minutely its construction, I give another description: 'This splendid vessel has been built on two large canoes, and is covered with the richest carving and gilding. This also, when used, will be drawn by war boats. In the centre is a lofty tower with eight or nine square storeys or terraces of black and gold, surmounted by the *tee*, or umbrella. The prows of the two canoes on which this water palace is constructed consist each of an immense silver dragon; and behind each dragon is the fierce colossal figure of a warrior deity called by the Burmese a Nut, but which is evidently identical with one of the Devatas of Hindoo mythology, of whom Indra is the special type. The stems of the canoes are beautifully adorned with a fretted work consisting of small pieces of looking-glass, which has a very rich appearance.' We returned to the house through the suburbs, and after a rest of half an hour I reluctantly took leave of the kind Chinaman, who had devoted so much time to my service, entertaining me most hospitably at his own house, and rode back to the steamer, feeling rather exhausted, but much gratified at the novel and wonderful experiences of the day.

CHAPTER VIII.

BHAMO AND THE OLD TRADE ROUTE

At daylight the next morning we started to remeasure the seven hundred miles of water communication between Mandalay and Rangoon. The river Irrawaddy is navigable as far as *Bhamo*, three hundred miles above the capital, and a steamer runs there once a month. On an island somewhere in this part of the river there is a Budhist monastery where are some large tame fish —fed regularly by the monks—which will come to the surface of the water at the simple cry of ' Tit-tit-tit.' They are said to be a large species of dog-fish, without scales, from three to five feet in length, and appear to consist chiefly of head and mouth. They are exceedingly voracious, and beg by the simple process of opening their huge jaws. These strange fish are so thoroughly domesticated as to freely permit anyone to stroke them on the back.

The scenery from Mandalay to Bhamo is said to be very fine, the river passing through narrow mountain gorges, fertile lands, and by picturesque villages, pagodas, and temples. Not far below *Bhamo* there is an especially striking and beautiful gorge or defile about fifteen miles in length. The river is there quite narrow, while the banks on either side rise to a height of five or six hundred feet, and are covered with grand old forests, which cast their dark shadows upon the smooth water. A huge rock—called 'Monkey Castle,' from the number of monkeys that hang about it—rising perpendicularly eight hundred feet above the surface of the river, is a noticeable feature of this wonderful defile. As the steamer slowly tugs along there is constant change in the view. Sometimes the river takes a winding course between the high and precipitous banks, with their dense green forests. At other places one comes upon a long vista of wood and stream. Here and there is a pagoda, or a village, or a few fishermen in a boat. The scene is not so much calculated to please and astonish the eye by wild sublimity, by rude precipices, as by graceful hills, glass-like water, and soft shadows.

This part of Burma is much the richest in its natural productions; the hills *contain* iron, coal, tin, copper, lead, gold, and silver—more than a million and a half dollars' worth of these two latter metals has been dug from the mines near Yunan, on the frontiers of China—sulphur, nitre, marble, and amber, and are *covered* (the hills) with valuable teak and oak timber; the topaz, ruby, sapphire, amethyst, and other gems are found in the beds of rivulets; while the valleys and plains offer, with moderate cultivation (the soil being remarkably fertile), millet, maize, wheat, cotton, tobacco, and the sugarcane. The produce of earth-oil (petroleum) in wells, some of them three hundred feet in depth, along the banks of the Irrawaddy is very great, amounting to more than eight million pounds per annum.

The *old* trade route between Burma and western China lay through Dhamo, but for the past twenty years it has been closed, owing to a rebellion in the province of Yunan (China). It appears that some Mussulman Chinese, called Panthays, suddenly broke out in rebellion, defeated the Chinese authorities and troops sent against them, and established themselves in a separate colony, with Tali-foo for their capital city and the residence of their king, who is styled 'Suleiman the First.' But although the Chinese cannot muster in sufficient force to put down these rebels, still they are continually harassing them, carrying on a 'dacoity war;' they devastate the country, keep the roads closed, and thus destroy commerce; and not until the Panthay

Government is acknowledged as actually established by the Emperor of China, and order and law are restored, will the old caravans with silks, cotton cloths, tea, earthenware, and ornamental articles find their way again down to Bhamo.

Within the last ten years various parties have investigated, and some have surveyed, different trade routes between Burma and China; but no further action has as yet been taken by the Burman Government than to subsidise a monthly line of steamers to Bhamo, from which place to the Shan States on the frontiers of China, the distance is about fifty miles 'as the crow flies.' One of the intended lines of overland communication between Burma and China is deserving of passing attention. It has been proposed to build a railway from Rangoon, four hundred miles, to a town called *Kiang-hung* on the great Makong river, from which the distance is only about twenty miles to the borders of Yunan. But it seems this could hardly prove a success; for were the route opened, then there would be the competition of easier and of course cheaper communication by water with Saigon and the French settlements; still the railway may yet be built, and at no very distant day. It is quite as feasible a project as many others of like nature which have been undertaken in different countries of Asia. India, among many other countries, has one continuous road extending from Calcutta to Peshawur, on the confines of Afghanistan, which is *more than sixteen hundred miles in length*; and already we hear of railroads in the islands of Java and Japan.

Bhamo itself is described as being a very ordinary-looking village, containing some four or five thousand inhabitants—Chinese, Shans, and Burmese. An English assistant political agent resides there, and is, I believe, the only European in the town. The former trade of Bhamo—silks, woollens, and cotton—was carried on principally by the Chinese, who arrived there from Yunan in large caravans during the months of December and January. "Under existing circumstances Bhamo has been dwindling away. History has repeated here in this remote quarter precisely what has befallen the great cities of the ancient world. When the Romans obtained possession of the Mediterranean trade, Tyre and Sidon passed into nothingness; when the land route through the Arabian desert was abandoned for the water route through the Red Sea, Petra and Edom became a howling wilderness. Whether Bhamo is to become a mere fishing village, or is once again to become an emporium of trade, depends upon whether the Panthays and Chinese can become friendly neighbours." There have been but few trips made by the English steamers, and no goods, excepting some cottons, have as yet passed either way. By the contract the steamers are obliged to carry down to Rangoon fifty deck passengers (emigrants) free of charge; on our passage we had fifty-three of them. They were all Shans or Laos, and were much fairer in complexion and stouter and stronger in body than the Burmese; moreover they spoke a different language.

The Laos race—estimated at 1,500,000 in number—inhabits a great part of the interior of the Hindoo-Chinese peninsula, and is divided into numerous tribes, some of which are subject to the Emperor of China, some owe a sort of dubious allegiance to the Kings of Ava, or Siam, or Annam, while very many are politically independent, being only under the government of their patriarchal chiefs. The Laos are a quiet, peaceable, and indolent people. They cultivate the soil, confining their attention chiefly to rice, though tobacco and sugar-cane and some vegetables are also grown; they manufacture beautifully lacquered wares, gold and silver ornaments, and silk for home consumption; they are also expert miners, their territory abounding in gold, silver, iron, and copper. The Laos tributaries of the

King of Ava export many cattle to Mandalay—these are small but useful, being strong and docile. The Ava Government adopts a rather curious though quite effectual (as it proves) method of compelling obedience from their Laos dependants. It seems that the latter are indebted to the former—their rulers—for so great a necessity of diet as suet, and the moment one of their chiefs proves refractory the supply is withheld until he shall implicitly yield what is enjoined.

In going down the river we stopped first at the town of *Tsagaing*, and took on board 1,000 baskets of grain (coarse peas, usually food for cattle), 1,000 baskets of wheat, and 200 hides. An amusing fact is connected with the hide trade. The Burmese are strictly forbidden by their religion to kill bullocks, cows, or calves; and yet, the captain tells me, sometimes as many as 5,000 hides are shipped at a time from one town. Besides, the King had even recently forbidden the European residents at Mandalay to slaughter any cattle within the royal dominions. Late in the afternoon we stopped at a small village called *Shoay-Ponk-Bew*, and remained there during the night, lading 2,500 baskets of grain, and on the following day we completed our cargo by receiving on board, at one village, 200 bales of loose and pressed cotton and 315 bags of *cutch* (a resinous product from which a valuable dye is manufactured), and at another village 900 baskets more of grain.

The steamer remained about six hours at *Thayet-myo*, and I embraced the opportunity to visit the English cantonment, stationed on the very frontier. It is nearly a mile from the native village, is well laid out, with good roads, and the barracks are built of wood, with shingle roofs, and are raised from the ground on brick, or stone, or plaster piles. The term of service for troops stationed here is usually four years. There is a small fort at *Thayet-myo*, which would be much strengthened were some works erected on the opposite side of the river, and to forward this project General Norman—the military member of the Viceroy's Council—had been recently sent from Calcutta. The General, returning home, became our fellow-passenger as far as Rangoon. He mentioned meeting the Hon. William H. Seward on the occasion of his recent visit to Calcutta (when making the tour of the world), and spoke very highly of the superior abilities and cordial affability of our renowned and venerated patriot and statesman.

On several evenings during the downward passage, our steamer was struck by furious squalls of wind, the

rain falling in torrents, but unaccompanied by either
thunder or lightning. These squalls were the harbingers of the change of monsoon—from north-east to
south-west in May—and after this change the rainy
season commences, and continues for four or five months.
It had been my intention to go from Rangoon to
Maulmain, and thence to travel overland to Bangkok in
Siam. The latter trip is neither difficult nor long. There
is a 'pass' through the Shan mountains (none of the
peaks of which rise above 8,200 feet in height), and elephants, ponies, and guides are easily procured. Leaving
the Shan mountains behind, one soon arrives at the Meklong river, where communication is easy with Bangkok
by boat, down the stream, and then fifty miles on a canal;
or one might travel nearly due east from Maulmain
until the great Menam was reached, and then sail
down this rapid stream, by the ancient capital of
Ayathia, to the modern capital, with its thousands of
floating houses and hundreds of graceful pagodas. But
this is a trip which, though easily possible from
November to April, still would be almost impossible
during the remaining months of the year, for sometimes
as many as ten and even twelve inches of rain fall
during one day in that part of Burma.

We stayed four hours at *Prome*—a town which resembles Mandalay in many respects. *Prome* was the seat of government for nearly five hundred years, but none of the Burmese kings have resided there since 1,000 B.C.

Nothing more of interest occurred on our downward voyage. We reached Rangoon on the 28th inst., just three weeks from the date of my departure 'up the Irrawaddy' for Mandalay.

CHAPTER IX.

FROM MAULMAIN AND PENANG

ANOTHER WEEK, passed in the chief city of British Burma, was made very pleasant for us by the good offices of the several residents we had first met as strangers, but whom we afterwards came to recognise as kind friends, and then we took passage in the British India Steam Navigation Co.'s steamer 'Mahratta,' 500 tons burden, Captain Lang in command, for Singapore, intending to stop at the towns of Maulmain, Penang, and Malacca on the passage. We were but twenty hours in descending the Rangoon river, crossing the bight of the Gulf of Martaban, and sighting the thickly-wooded promontory beyond the little village of *Amherst*, which latter was formerly the capital of the Tenasserim provinces, but is now only used as a pilot station. Near Amherst may be seen the lonely grave of Mrs. Judson, the devoted missionary and wife, shaded by a single beautiful *hopea* tree. We had entered the *Salween* river—one of the largest in that remote part of the world—and a rapid run of twenty-seven miles brought us to *Maulmain*, and we dropped anchor abreast of the business quarter of the town, with but a half-dozen small vessels in sight. The town does not appear to advantage from the river, almost hidden as it is by immense groves of the cocoa-nut and betel-nut palm, banana, papaya, bamboo, and other tropical plants. The population, comprising Burmese, Chinese, Parsees, Armenians, Klings, Jews, and Cingalese, is about 10,000; the European residents may number less than a hundred.

There are many large timber-yards at Maulmain; indeed, it has always been famed for its export of teak logs which are cut in the forests upon the banks of the Salween, and then floated, sometimes hundreds of miles, down to the capital. In these timber-yards the usefulness, power, sagacity, and docility of the elephant is most wonderfully illustrated, for these uncouth monsters are employed in drawing, stacking, and shifting the immense teak logs—some of them weighing as much as two tons. A log that *forty* coolies could scarcely move the elephant will quietly lift upon his tusks, and holding it there with his proboscis, will carry it to whatever part of the yard he may be directed by his driver. They will also, using trunk, feet, and tusks, pile the huge timbers as evenly and correctly as one could wish. What surprised us the most was to see the elephants select and pick out particular timbers from the centre of an indiscriminate stack or heap of

ELEPHANT EMPLOYED IN A TIMBER-YARD, MAULMAIN

more than a hundred simply at the command of the driver. The huge beasts are directed by the *mahouts*, or drivers, by spoken orders, pressure of the feet on their necks, and the customary use of the *ankus*, or elephant goad. It usually requires a year or a year and a half to teach them the 'lumber business,' and when thoroughly taught they are worth from Rs. 500 upwards, according to their abilities. We saw one, a venerable old fellow nearly ten feet in height, for which the owner said he had refused an offer of Rs. 3,000. Sometimes an animal breaks his tusks, being forced to carry an excessive weight by a stupid or brutal driver; though the elephant knows his own power, and generally refuses to lift more than his tusks can safely bear, for if these should be broken off close to the head, death would soon ensue; if only cracked they are hooped about with iron bands, and are thus rendered serviceable for many years.

On leaving Maulmain our course was nearly due south. We saw, though dimly, some of the islands of the *Mergui Archipelago*, belonging to the British, and the island of *Junk Ceylon*, which has extensive tin mines, and which exports the famous edible birds' nests, eaten as a luxury by the Chinese. Soon afterward we obtained glimpses of the Malay peninsula— the Golden Chersonese of the ancients. The sea life of our Chinese passengers was to us a diverting spectacle, and greatly relieved what would otherwise have been a rather monotonous voyage. Some of them were 'saloon' passengers, and ate at our table. They wore the orthodox blue shirt and baggy trousers, slippers and 'pigtails,' and long finger-nails—one gentleman in particular had these useful appendages nearly as long as his fingers—and they smoked tobacco and opium in little brass pipes, and gambled through half of the night. They seemed intelligent, and were very dignified at table, partaking, of everything, and using their knife and fork, gracefully. By going 'forward' we could see the 'deck' passengers, a lower class, eating with *chop-sticks*—little pieces of wood the size of lead pencils, and about eight inches in length, held between the thumb and forefinger, and supported by the second and third fingers—from numerous little bowls. Their food consisted o rice and little fishes, or bits of pork, or potted duck, and fruit, though shrimps, crabs, potatoes and squashes are also eaten by them; very weak tea was drunk between meals, and at meals usually nothing, though sometimes I detected a bottle of so-called 'champagne.' 'John Chinaman' lives temperately, though he has pretty exact ideas upon the subject of good living. On the steamer they cooked with small portable charcoal furnaces; usually each variety of food was kept by itself in a separate bowl, though sometimes stews of everything, all the 'odds and ends,' well mixed, were made. A Chinaman eats from many little bowls, holding one of rice in his hand, and selecting bits from the others in turn to mix and eat with the rice; in

A BUDDHIST PRIEST

eating, they hold the bowl to the lips, and then poke the food into their mouths with the chop-sticks. They ate but twice a day, and at the conclusion of a meal most amusing was it to see all the dishes washed in about half a pint of water.

Our voyage was much 'lightened' also by the society and friendship of the Right Rev. T. Bigandet, Bishop of Rangoon and Apostolic Vicar of Ava and Pegu. He is a talented and pleasant old gentleman, and was proceeding to Penang, for the purpose of ordaining a young priest there. The reverend father has lived twelve years in Penang and about the same time in Burma, and has travelled over nearly all the country between Calcutta and Singapore. He speaks eight languages, including the difficult Burmese, Malay, and Hindustani. He has written a very learned work on the ethnology of the Burmese, another on the life of Gaudama, the ways to Neibban, and the *phongyees* or monks, and is altogether the best informed gentleman concerning those strange countries and their stranger peoples that we had the pleasure of meeting.

At daylight on the morning of the 10th of May we were awakened by the steward, who whispered through the keyhole of the door of our cabin, 'Penang is in sight, gentlemen.' We dressed quickly, and going on deck, there we beheld the beautiful little island, scarcely two miles distant. A sudden rain squall came on, hiding everything from view, but we were soon anchored off Fort Cornwallis, and a notice was posted on the main-deck that the 'Mahratta'

would remain thirty hours, thus giving ample time for
'through' passengers to land. An English war vessel,
a small Siamese steamer, and a half-dozen ships of
various nationalities lay at anchor near by, while
farther to the southward were about a hundred Chinese
junks. The strait in which we were anchored was
about two miles wide, and *Palo Penang*, covered with
cocoa and areca palms, (its name is derived from the
latter, *Penang* being the Malay word for the betel-nut
palm, and *Palo* meaning island; it is also sometimes
called Prince of Wales' Island), nutmeg and clove
trees, dorians, and all the Malayan fruits, lay before us.
It is fifteen miles in length and eight in width. The
eastern part consists of a large plain, two or three miles
in depth, and on the western side of the island there is
a range of granite hills which rise in one place to a
height of 2,500 feet, where there is a signal station, and
some European *bungalows*, or country houses. Penang
was purchased in 1785 by the East India Company
from the Rajah of Queda, a neighbouring Malay prince,
for 2,000 Spanish dollars. At that time the island was
without a single inhabitant; now it has a population
of 60,000—Malays, Chinese, natives of India, other
Asiatics, and Europeans, about 200 of the latter.
On the mainland opposite Penang is a strip of country,

sixty miles in length and twenty in breadth, purchased
by the British in 1802, and called Province Wellesley;
its population numbers 50,000, mostly Malays, who
raise large quantities of sugar-cane for export. At one
time black pepper was largely grown by the Chinese
in Penang, but now Sumatra and some other East
Indian islands have taken the lead in this valuable
commodity. Penang forms, together with Province
Wellesley, Malacca, and Singapore, what is called the
Straits Settlements, the government being under the
direction of the Lieutenant-Governor of Singapore,
who formerly was subject to the Viceroy of India,
but latterly, I believe, now reports directly to the
(English) Home Government.

The town—once called George Town—lies upon the
north-eastern corner of the island. We are rowed
ashore in a *sampan*—a small passenger row-boat—by a
smiling Chinaman, who wears an immense hat, shaped
like a sugar-bowl cover, made of palm leaf, and a coat
or short cape made of rope, waterproof, and which
strikingly resembles a western door-mat. Landing at
the stone jetty, we enter a *gharry,* the regulation cab
of the east, and are driven through some of the principal streets. Chinese *sampans,* as well as junks, all
have huge eyes painted upon their prows, for, says

'John,' 'Spose no hab got eyes, how can see?' which terse explanation should certainly satisfy the most inquisitive. Riding along a broad and clean street, we noticed a few fine squares, though there were no public edifices of any particular beauty; the private dwellings of the Europeans were pleasantly situated in the midst of fine gardens. Very many of the streets were occupied by Chinese shops; among them we noticed those in which the liquors *shamshu* and *bhang* (strong spirits made from rice and hemp) were dispensed; there were also many *joss* or idol houses to be seen. A regiment of sepoys is stationed here; the small fort commands the town and harbour, and just courts and an excellent police organisation combine to preserve order even with such a mixed population.

The great fertility of Penang is owing to the high temperature of its climate, together with the moisture produced by so great an extent of surrounding water; and it is perhaps a more healthy residence for Europeans than any lowland station in India. When one is worn with sickness or the cares of business, it is only necessary to go from the plains to the hills, eight miles distant, to find a perfect *sanitarium*, with a temperature which ranges from 70° to 75° Fahrenheit throughout the year. We had fortunately abundant time to visit 'Penang Mountain.' In our *gharry* we rode four miles to the foot of the hills, and ordered two grooms with ponies to follow us for the steeper half—the remaining four miles of the journey. The road is very good, and runs past the foreign residences; then ensue immense plantations of cocoa and areca palms, with little Malay huts embedded in them; groves of bread-fruit trees, nutmegs, cloves, bananas, bamboos, and the pepper-plant follow; then again we pass cocoa palms—millions of them; and finally the *gharry* halts alike at the terminus of the road and the foot of the hills, and from here it is but a half-mile to a wonderful waterfall. In the midst of dense woods a mountain torrent, about twenty feet in width, dashes down a precipice of jagged stone, at least a hundred and fifty feet in height, and falls, with a noise of thunder, into a small, deep pool, whence it flows on down the hill in a channel deeply cut through the solid rock. The fall is a grand sight now at the end of the dry season, but must be much grander after the annual rains, when the water is said to fall in a nearly solid sheet. On one side of this fall, at the bottom, there is a small Hindoo temple—a singular example of the reverence which even pagans have for the sublime in nature. From this mountain torrent large iron pipes convey cool water to Penang, far away off on the heated plain.

Our ponies had now arrived, and, mounted on their backs, we commenced the ascent of the hills by an excellent bridle-path. After a ride of about two miles, winding backwards and forwards over the hills and through the valleys, but continually rising higher, we reached a region of beautiful ferns, interlaced vines, and huge trees, having trunks over a hundred feet in height, straight 'as an arrow,' and with but few branches, and these near their tops, and so thickly set with their foliage that the brightest noonday sun could scarcely penetrate them. Occasionally we obtained glimpses of the plains and sea below, but not until we had reached the signal station did the magnitude and magnificence of the view burst upon us. The flag-staff is about 2,500 feet above the sea-level, and scattered around on convenient heights near at hand are some dozen *bungalows*, including a large and comfortable one belonging to the Governor. The view from the observatory was simply superb. Away to the north was the ocean, dotted by little green islands, and the peninsula of Malacca, with its level plains close to it, and ranges of mountains—some peaks over a mile in height—afar off; to the east lay the town of

Penang, the houses with red tiled roofs, and white and yellow walls, the bright emerald groves of tropical trees, and the well-made roads, and the sea with hundreds of vessels at anchor; then beyond, on the mainland, were perfect forests of cocoa palms, and a small river, shining like molten silver, wending away to the mountains, whose dim outlines could just be discerned in the distance; to the south were some islands covered with the rankest of vegetation, and the eye also looked over the beautiful hills and valleys of Penang island itself; while to the westward lay the azure-hued ocean stretching away, in calm majesty, to the horizon.

The air was so pure and exhilarating that we walked the greater part of the distance to the foot of the hills without fatigue, and then, re-entering our *gharry*, returned to the steamer, first purchasing, however, some *dorians* and *mangosteens*, the former fruit being largely grown in Penang. The *mangosteen* is about the size of a Sicily orange, and grows upon a small tree which much resembles the orange tree. The skin is a reddish brown, like that of the egg-plant; the rind is red, bitter, and about a third of an inch thick, and within it is a white pulp, divided into six or eight parts, each with a large seed. The flavour is very much like that of wild grapes, vinous and refreshing. On eating it the rind is broken with the fingers, and then the white pulp is removed with a fork or spoon. The *mangosteen* is justly esteemed the most delicious of the East Indian fruits. We had often heard of the exquisite flavour though disagreeable smell of the *dorian*, so we resolved to taste one of them and judge for ourselves. This fruit is much the shape of, though the size is larger than a pineapple; it is green and covered with short thorns; the husk is yellow, and about a third of an inch in thickness; within the pulp is divided into four quarters, each with a central rib or partition, and six large seeds the size and shape of hen's eggs, which are covered with the thin, juicy, edible matter. The smell of the *dorian* when first opened is like *stale fish*, and when eaten the flavour is like *raw onions*, leaving a nauseating *garlic* taste in the mouth. However, notwithstanding its rank odour, many Europeans resident in the east profess to like the *dorian*, but we thought its beginning, intervening, and final taste most unsavoury, nay, even extremely disgusting.

On leaving Penang we had fairly entered the *Straits of Malacca*—a channel 500 miles in length, which connects the China Sea with the Indian Ocean, flowing between the Malay peninsula and the island of Sumatra, with a width of from 25 to 200 miles, and steamed along in sight of land, on one hand or on the other, the greater part of the time. The navigation of some part of the straits is difficult and dangerous for heavy draught vessels, there being huge sandbanks which extend across it, leaving only narrow, tortuous channels. We passed several large ships and two or three 'canalers,' steamers bound for different European ports, *viâ* the Suez Canal. On the morning of the 13th we sighted the old town of *Malacca*, and were soon after at anchor about three miles from the shore.

CHAPTER X.

TO MALACCA AND SINGAPORE.

THE town of Malacca, founded in the year 1252, was taken by the Portuguese under Albuquerque in 1511, by the Dutch in 1641, and by the English in 1695; again held by the Dutch from 1818 to 1825, when, with an adjacent territory extending for forty miles along the coast and thirty miles inland, it was ceded to Britain in exchange for Bencoolen, in Sumatra. Of late years Malacca has much declined; whereas formerly it contained 20,000 inhabitants, there are now but 13,000—two-thirds of which number are Malays. The trade is mostly in the hands of the Chinese; there are not many Europeans, and none engaged in trade; a few only are in the Government service. From our anchorage the little native town looks very pretty, and the European residences upon a small hill and an old church nearly covered with trees can just be discerned. To the right of the town, though thirty miles inland, lies *Nit. Ophir*, a single peak 5,700 feet high, rising sharply from the plain, and the locality where there is mined a good quantity of gold. About the same distance to the left are some excellent tin mines.

In the middle of the day, going on shore with the captain, the first objects which attracted our attention were the ruined churches, and the original fortifications built by Albuquerque, immediately behind the town upon a hill about a hundred feet in height. The ruins are those of the Portuguese monasteries of St. Paul and of the *Hermanas de leche* with the church of *Madre de Dios*, in which once reposed the ashes of the celebrated apostle of the Indies, St. Francis Xavier, which were afterwards transferred to Goa. We saw a tomb slab within the crumbling walls, carved with an hour-glass and wings, death's head and cross bones, and bearing the date 1568, all in good preservation. One part of this church is now used as a signal station, and another as a powder magazine. We afterwards noticed in the town several tall, many-storied dwellings of the architecture of the 16th century. Entering a *gharry*, we were driven to the old cemetery, where sleep many thousand Chinese far from their 'flowery kingdom.' The grounds embrace a hill about a mile in circumference, and upon its sloping sides all the graves have been dug; there are no divisions between the stones, which are low, carved with Chinese characters, and sometimes gilded or coloured red or green. Chinese graves have no footstones, and the head stone is always placed towards the bottom of the hill, and around the remainder of the grave there runs a low horseshoe-shaped wall, built even with the turf on its outer side.

The vegetation of Malacca is, like that of Penang, very luxuriant. The streets of the town are clean, though not broad or straight. The Chinese houses are well made, two storeys in height, and as we rode along we generally saw, through the open doors, that they contained mineral paintings of some one of their numerous gods. We took 'tiffin' (lunch) with an old Portuguese resident, born in Malacca, and the agent of the steamship company to which the 'Mahratta' belongs. In conversation afterwards the old gentleman told me that he acted the part of 'the good Samaritan' to the destitute captain and officers of one of the American ships which the piratical Captain Semmes plundered and burned almost within sight of Singapore, and then brought into Malacca. Returning to the steamer, we weighed anchor at four o'clock in the afternoon, and at daybreak on the following morning had passed the southern extremity of the peninsula of Malacca, and were in sight of the island of Singapore, which is low, richly wooded, with very irregular shores, and skirted by beautiful little islands, the homes of native fishermen. Like Malacca, very little of the town or city of Singapore appears from the sea, though a hill, with a signal-staff and the Governor's house, and a long row of well-built *godowns* (stores or warehouses), stand rather prominently forth. We steam past two or three war vessels, two telegraph steamers (which are only awaiting orders from London to commence laying a wire from here to Hong Kong), and by some thirty or forty merchant ships of all nations to our anchorage in the crescent-shaped roadstead about a mile from the town. We engage a Malay *prow* to take us ashore, and are landed near the *Hotel d'Europe*, to which our good captain has recommended us. This hotel we find to be very large and comfortable, situated in the midst of beautiful gardens, facing 'the green,' and commanding a fine view of the straits, the large island of Bintang in the distance, and the Chinese junks and foreign shipping in the harbour. Attached to the establishment, which is kept by a German, is that 'peculiar institution' an American bar-room, where California mixed drinks are served, and there is besides a 'regular down east Boston Arctic soda-water fountain;' a billiard-room;

and a reading-room, where one will find papers and journals, in four or five languages, from New York, London, Bombay, Calcutta, Batavia, Hong Kong, Shanghae, Yokohama, and San Francisco.

The island of Singapore, situated but eighty miles north of the equator, and separated from the mainland by a strait less than a mile in width, is itself about twenty-seven miles in length by fifteen in breadth, and no part of its surface rises more than 500 feet above the sea-level. *Gutta-percha*, the prepared juice of a tree, was originally discovered in this island; the principal products are now spices, sugar-cane, and fruits; the only important manufacture is that of sago, which, however, comes from the eastern parts of the Malay Archipelago. Singapore, taken by the British in 1818, was, six years subsequently, confirmed in their possession by treaty with the native Malay prince—the Sultan of Johore—to whom it had belonged. The town of Singapore is situated on the south-east corner of the island. The term Singapore or Singapura, is derived from the Sanscrit, *singa*, a lion, and *pura*, a town, Lion-town, or 'town of lions,' though why so fancifully named is not known; there are no lions in the island, the nearest approach to the 'king of beasts' being his royal cousin the Bengal tiger. Formerly these latter animals made sad havoc among the natives; a man a day, on an average, was killed for many years after the founding of the settlement. The wily beasts were said to swim across the channel from the adjacent continent, where they were quite plentiful, and on this account it was thought impossible to rid the island of their presence; but by cutting down and burning the jungle and building towns the annual death-rate has decreased to about a dozen a year, and these are usually coolies, who are employed in the spice and other plantations in the interior, far away from any dwellings.

The present population of the island is nearly 100,000, of which number 60,000 are Chinese and about 6,000 Europeans. Singapore is said, for its size, to have the most conglomerate population of any city in the world. It is a free port, and consequently has a large trade. It owes its present prosperity, and even existence, to the fact of its being situated upon the great thoroughfare of eastern commerce; ships can be found at this great *entrepôt* of spices, pepper, sago, rattan, coirrope, oil, etc., loading for all parts of the world; it is a coaling station for the men-of-war of all nations, and the India and China lines of steamers make it a port; it is a great commercial emporium in which are warehoused for future distribution the staple products of America, Europe, and Asia. Fifty years ago even, Crawford — at one time Governor of the settlement—said that Singapore had become the great *entrepôt* of south Asia and the Malay Archipelago, to which the inhabitants of all parts of the Indian Ocean resorted with the produce of their farming and manufacturing industry, and in which they found a ready market abundantly stocked with every variety of European goods.

During our stay at Singapore we received every kindness and attention from the American Consul, Dr. Jewell, of Washington, D.C., who lived with his wife in the same hotel. Dr. J. and his family are Mississippians by birth, education, and residence, but they remained faithfully loyal to the National Government during our late terrible civil war. The Doctor has been seventeen years in Washington, connected, in various capacities, with both the Treasury and Post-Master General's Departments. He had lived a little more than two years in Singapore, and was both able and willing to give us much valuable information.

One day we visited Fort Canning to obtain a general view of Singapore. This fort, built upon a small pyramid-shaped hill, about 200 feet in height, and just back of the town, mounts, among numerous guns of smaller calibre, some few 68-pounders, and is garrisoned by 300 British and 700 Sepoy troops. Singapore is divided into a Malay, Chinese, and European 'town,' or quarter; it is too irregular to present a handsome appearance, but the view of the shipping in the harbour and the distant islands is rather impressive. The town is divided by a small river, in which are thousands of native craft of every description, many of them being employed as lighters in the harbour. On the extreme western side lies the Chinese quarter; nearer is the European business town, the centre of which is laid out in a small garden or park, around which is a narrow street faced by two strong brick stores, and called 'Commercial Square.' To the east of the river are the public buildings, the esplanade, chief hotels, European residences, and the greater part of the Kling community. In this quarter of the town is a handsome building styled the 'Singapore Institution,' furnished with a library, museum, branch schools, &c., for the cultivation of the Chinese and Malay languages and literatures; it was established by Sir Stamford Raffles, the founder of the settlement of Singapore, in 1823. The Governor's house is a large brick and stucco building on the summit of a little knoll, perhaps half a mile inland from Fort Canning. Were it not for its immense cupola it would be mistaken for a Government department or office of some kind, and, as it is, the second storey, composed entirely of arches and Venetian blinds, and the upper storey formed of pillars and Venetians, present a very ugly appearance. There are few trees about the house, so that it receives the entire force of both sun and rain, and, excepting only when a strong breeze is blowing, it must be a very uncomfortable residence.

The large Chinese temple of Singapore is worthy of a visit. It is situated in one of the principal streets, and consists of a plain stone house with most fantastic and curious adornments, having a court-yard in front and around open sheds. Before the entrance there two large stone tigers, in whose mouths held by the teeth, may be seen and felt, perfectly round, loose stones, so cut out by an ingenious Chinaman. Then there are bas-reliefs, and inscriptions, and figures carved upon the front of the building, while its pillars are encircled by enormous dragons. But it is in the supporting of the roof that the most lavish ornamentation is to be seen—the wood carving of gods, and animals, and flowers, and arabesques, all painted and gilded, being something wonderful. In the interior of the large building are three niches, and in these sit three gods, each about a foot in height, carved in wood and richly gilded; and before them are altars upon which burn a peculiar kind of punk, or slow-match, and candles, and there are besides fruits and rice, placed as votive offerings. On these altars there were also *wishing-blocks*—pieces of wood five inches by three, shaped like kidney-beans, and finely carved. In 'wishing' they are held by one extremity, side by side in the hands, and then thrown in the air, the manner of their falling indicating good or evil fortune; but I have heard somewhere that the ingenious people have a knack of throwing them until they fall in the desired way. Near the wishing-blocks upon the altar were huge metallic cups, containing each about fifty little thin sticks of bamboo. Each of these sticks has a number upon it, which indicates a passage in their 'Book of Moral Sentences,' and the Chinamen shake the cups round until one of these little sticks falls out, and if the reference to this should not prove satisfactory, why, they simply shake again, and so on. Some of the idols resembled jolly old mandarins, but most had a very disagreeable look, with their narrow, almond-shaped eyes, broad, sensual faces, and thick, flabby lips. The interior of this temple was covered with the most flaring red and black Chinese texts, and

THE FAN PALM.—THE TRAVELLERS FOUNTAIN.

the roofs were ornamented with little dragons, made of encaustic tiles and glass.

We next visited the market, which contained a great variety of vegetables and fruits, but few meats, the Chinese diet consisting principally of fish and pork. We drove several times, while in Singapore, into the interior of the island, *via* Orchard Road and River Valley Road, on which are situated the European bungalows, or country houses, from two to four miles from town. Orchard Road seems to be the most popular as a residence. After leaving town it passes through a narrow valley, with a series of little hillocks on either hand, and upon which many houses have been built. The road is very pretty, being lined by tall bamboo hedges and trees which, uniting above, form a complete shade; the beautiful *fan-palm*—or 'traveller's fountain,' as it is sometimes called—will deserve especial notice, with its immense spread of feathery leaves, constituting an exact semicircle. The bungalows are generally built of brick and stucco, like those of India, and are surrounded by large compounds, or gardens. The vegetation is always in the full bloom of summer in Singapore, owing to its proximity to the equator and the almost daily showers of rain. Beyond the residences are the remains of many nutmeg plantations (the nutmeg for some reason or other will not flourish in Singapore), then succeeds a strip of thin jungle, then the Chinese pepper and gambier plantations, and then comes the jungle in earnest, with its gigantic trees, creepers, orchids, parasites, and fallen or decayed trees, plants, and vegetables. A very beautiful spot near Singapore is called New Harbour. The harbour consists of a long row of wharves, about three miles from town, where the Peninsular and Oriental and the *Messageries Maritimes* steamers lie, and where there are coal sheds, and docks built for their repair. New Harbour is nearly land-locked by many beautiful little green islands, and the clear blue water and the graceful hills of Singapore add to the charm of the scene.

Cocoa-nut oil is a large item of export from Singapore. Dr. Little, an English gentleman and an old resident, to whom I was so fortunate as to bring letters of introduction, called one morning at the hotel to take me in his buggy to a large cocoa-nut plantation, owned partly by himself and five miles distant from the town. The estate is nearly a mile square, embracing about six hundred acres, situated near the sea shore, and the soil, at least as far as the roots penetrate, is entirely composed of sand. The trees are planted in rows each way about twenty feet apart, and are of all ages and sizes. Cocoa-nuts are raised principally for their oil, though rope is made from their husks, and some quantity of them is exported for food. We walked for some time beneath the trees, and then, re-entering the buggy, drove to a distant part of the plantation where there was a coir-rope manufactory. The European manager was kind enough to explain the different processes of manufacture, which are extremely simple. First the cocoa-nuts are broken in halves, and the meat is grated off the shells and boiled down to make oil, while the husks are soaked for a day or two in a large tank of water. When taken from the tank they are quite soft, and their coats are then removed by simply forcing them between and through two rough rollers (revolving by steam); this process leaves the long straight fibres, which are something like those of a broom, and next they are cleaned by being placed in a large fan-mill. The fibres are then taken to another house, where they are again cleaned by shaking them in the air with two sticks, and then they are ready to be spun into ropes of various sizes. There are several ingenious as well as simple contrivances for the twisting of the strands, though the greater part of the rope is made by hand. Nearly 200 Malays and Chinese were employed in this establishment, which 'turns out' about 25,000 pounds of rope per annum. This kind of rope, though extensively used by vessels, is not so strong as that made from hemp. We took a *chota hayree*, a little breakfast, with the obliging superintendent, and arrived in town again about nine o'clock, at the regular breakfast hour.

In the afternoon we rode to the house and gardens of the Hon. Mr. Whampoa, a Chinese merchant who, unlike the majority of his countrymen, has settled for life at Singapore, where he has been for a long time in business, and is reported to have made a fortune of $2,000,000. Mr. Whampoa is a well-educated gentleman, speaks English perfectly, and is a member of the town council. His house, three miles from the town, is a complete museum, filled with the most expensive and beautiful *curios* from all countries, while his gardens—he is a great lover of flowers—are one of the 'lions' of the place, and one of the first questions asked a stranger by the European residents of Singapore is, 'Have you seen the Chinaman's gardens? if not, be sure and do so before leaving.' These gardens are rather a work of art than nature, i.e. the most interesting plants to be seen have been brought to their present form and condition by the hand and skill of

man. Some shrubs—a species of box apparently—
are tortured into the most fantastic shapes by means of
clipping and confining them with wires. One may
see living dogs, dragons, fish, and exactly formed
boats, pagodas, and baskets. In many parts of the
gardens may be observed the monstrous *Victoria
Regia* lilies, here growing in the open air. Walking
along, we saw fish-ponds, summer-houses, canals,
hedges, a very network of paths, neatly gravelled, and
then we came to the—*pig-sty*, a long shed filled with
separate pens, or boxes, in which immense pigs, of
different breeds, were wallowing, one hog—nearly the
size of a cow—being too fat to stand upon its feet.

We also had an opportunity to see a sago manufactory through the kindness of Dr. Little, who sent
his Chinese servant, who spoke English, with us as
cicerone. It is not generally known that sago is the
pith of a tree called the sago palm. The raw product
comes chiefly from Borneo and Sumatra, and Singapore
is its chief place of manufacture and exportation. The
sago palm bears but once—in its fifteenth year—it is
then cut down, the pith is removed, cleared of its
fibres, pressed into small masses, and, being bound with
leaves, is shipped to the factory. Here it is washed a
number of times, dried, and passed through sieves,

becoming a fine white flour. It is then placed in large pieces of linen, sprinkled with water, and shook until it forms into grains; then it is dried in large kettles heated very hot, next passed through a fan-mill, and dried for a day on large mats placed in the sun, and then, being put in bags holding about two bushels, is ready for shipment as the sago of commerce. The factory consisted of a series of large open sheds, and the workmen were all Chinese. Chinamen are the industrious, hard-working class of the native population of Singapore; the Malays and Klings (from the Coromandel coast of India) are boatmen, *gharry wallahs* (cab drivers), sailors, *dhobees* (washermen), fishermen, &c.

It may give some idea of the remarkable produce of the sago palm when it is known that three trees will yield more nutritive matter than an acre of wheat, and six trees more than an acre of potatoes. And hence we find that sago is the sole bread of the inhabitants of the Spice Islands and Papua, or New Guinea, and its neighbouring islands.

GENERAL VIEW OF BANGKOK AND THE MENAM RIVER

CHAPTER XL

BANGKOK

At Singapore I parted from my English friend, he going to Ceylon, Bombay, and thence, *viâ* the Suez Canal, to London; and I to Java, and Japan, and China. In Yokohama it was my good fortune to meet the Baron Hübner—formerly ambassador of Austria in Paris and in Rome—and two English gentlemen, who were fresh from a fourteen months' tour through the United States. At the Baron's kind solicitation, I joined his party, and then we visited in turn Shanghae, Tientsin, Pekin, and the 'Great Wall.' But I cannot reproduce here the strange scenes we witnessed in northern China; nor can I relate how hospitably we were entertained by Ministers Low, Vlangalli, Calicé, and Wade in the 'Tartar City;' nor can I give an account of our voyage 600 miles up the great Yang-tse-Kiang river to Hankow and Wuchang; nor may I write about the quaint sights of Canton or Macao: all this would easily fill another volume, and besides the title-page speaks only of travels in Farther India. Merely let me add that from Hong Kong we crossed the China Sea to Manilla and the Philippine Islands, and then our course was towards the equator, to Saigon; and now again, seven months from the time of my departure, I find myself at the 'Hôtel de l'Europe,' Singapore, eager and impatient to visit those other lands of the White Elephant and the areca palm—Siam, Cambodia, and Cochin China.

My fellow-travellers having decided to go on to Ceylon and India, alone I go on board the steamer 'Martaban,' of 600 tons burden, which Capt. Buxton informs me will leave at nine o'clock in the evening for Bangkok. I find myself to be the only cabin passenger on board, and also soon find that the steamer is remarkably slow, making but about six knots per hour, and the distance to Bangkok being 800 miles, with the north-east monsoon blowing and a head current of a knot and a half running. Fortunately with pleasant weather we crossed the China Sea, and on December 30 entered the Gulf of Siam (500 miles in length by 250 in breadth), and which, notwithstanding the peninsula of Cambodia consists for the most part of low-lying land, is never visited by typhoons or heavy gales. The head of the gulf is a 'bight' about sixty miles square, and entering this, an island away to the north-east was the first land of Siam—the chief kingdom of the Chin-Indian group of countries—seen by the officers of the steamer. Soon after some hills upon the mainland to the westward of us appeared; and about four o'clock in the afternoon, with the lowland lying ahead and just visible, we received on board our pilot. At the mouth of the Menam river there is an almost impassable bar, a channel through which might easily be kept open, but the Siamese authorities object to such a project. It is reported that a few years ago some English merchants offered to dredge a channel through this bar, whereupon the King told them he would not have it done on any account, that rather he would prefer to pay somebody to place a sandbank there— that it was a good protection against enemies. And just at the mouth of the river the Siamese have sunk three junks, in the same enlightened spirit which prompts them to retain the bar intact; but the pilots, knowing the position of these junks, manage, though with difficulty, to pass between them. The river seems about half a mile in width; its banks are fringed with mangroves and jungle, and beyond are immense *paddy* fields.

About six miles up the river we came to the small village of Pakuam, where is the Siamese custom-house;

and two forts, the one on a small island opposite the town, mounting eight or ten large guns, the one next the town with no armament, and seeming to be in a very dilapidated condition. According to rule, the captain is compelled to anchor and land at the custom-house— a large bamboo shed, with a palm-leaf roof, and containing nothing but a table and two or three chairs. A Siamese official in native dress—a short white jacket and a strip of cloth around the waist and drawn between the thighs—presents a common blank-book, in which the captain writes his report, and besides (at the request of the officer, who spoke English fairly), some information concerning the movements of the King of Siam at Singapore. His Majesty was at the time absent from the kingdom on a pleasure excursion to Calcutta and India. Proceeding up the river, just above Pakunm we noticed another small fort having a few guns, but no guard or other evidence of occupation. Opposite this fort on an island is a plain white pagoda and some small temples; these are used only on particular festival days. The river banks are very beautiful, being thickly covered with the vegetation peculiar to the tropics— bamboos, bananas, cocoa palms, mangroves, and hundreds of plants of familiar form but unknown name. We next passed some immense sugar-cane plantations,

HIS MAJESTY THE KING OF SIAM

then some *paddy* fields and a Burmese village on the right, and orange gardens and a small town on the left bank. The river here doubles upon itself, so to speak, thus increasing the distance to Bangkok by fifteen miles. We afterwards passed large plains of betel-nut and cocoa-nut palms on the one side, and dock and ship-building yards upon the other. Owing to a low tide we anchor here, though the city proper is nearly two miles distant, and nothing can be seen of it, the ground being too level and the vegetation too dense. The captain takes me ashore in his gig. We pass on the right a French Roman Catholic church, another custom-house, and the Consulates of America, Germany, England, France, and Portugal. These consular buildings are plainly built of brick and stucco, situated in large compounds of plants and flowers near the river. In this section of the Menam are anchored many small barks, most of them flying the national standard of a white elephant on a crimson ground; no large vessels and no steamers are to be seen, though in commerce Bangkok once ranked second only to Calcutta and Canton.

We land at Falcks' 'Bowling Alley and Billiard Hall,' and enquire for rooms in the boarding and lodging department, which we find situated a short distance back from the river. 'Falcks' Hotel' consists of a long, low, one-storey building, raised upon piles about four feet from the ground, and I am shown by the polite proprietor into a room less than ten feet square, it being 'the best the house affords;' the sides of this room extend only to the eaves of the roof, the entire building being open above them to the ridgepole. The people assembled at dinner were all Germans, and apparently all skippers—masters of the merchant vessels in port. The table was graced by the presence of but one lady, a captain's wife. On the following day, being the bearer of a letter of introduction to the Private Secretary of the Supreme King—Nai phon Raya nat tianahar—I called upon the American Consul—General F. W. Partridge, of Illinois—to ask his advice concerning its disposal. Sending in my card, a tall and slender gentleman about sixty years of age, dressed in a white duck suit with gilt army buttons, soon presented himself, and gave me a most cordial greeting. Upon stating that, having no acquaintance there, I had taken the liberty to call and ask his advice concerning the things best worth seeing in Bangkok and the surrounding country, the General very kindly offered me any assistance in his power. The Private Secretary, to whom my letter was addressed, had gone with the King to Calcutta. The Consul—a truly representative American—graduated in the University of Vermont; was president for some time of a college in Pennsylvania; served in the Mexican war and through the greater part of the late civil war, and bears upon his body many scars—honourable proofs of fidelity and zeal in his country's cause. He has resided in Bangkok a little more than two years, and proposes remaining two more.

In the afternoon the Consul's son, who acted as U.S. Marshal, kindly took me to see something of the city. We went in the Consulate barge, which is simply a large row-boat of the gondola pattern, with a small pavilion in its centre fitted with blinds and shelves and seats and cushions; and the boatmen in livery, two behind and two before, row standing and facing the bow, looking forwards. Bangkok has been aptly styled the 'Venice of the East,' for its thoroughfares and highways of traffic are simply intersecting canals and branches of the river; and the majority of the houses are either floating, built upon rafts, or upon piles on the sides of these waterways. There are some narrow paths on *terra firma*, however, and the King has recently built a long stretch of road as a drive; it is reported that he also promises to build highways alongside of the principal canals. The situation of Bangkok is unique. The river Menam flows through its western quarter, and upon the eastern there is a wall fifteen feet in height and about twelve in breadth. When the capital was moved here from Ayuthia, in 1769, the houses were built upon the banks of the river, but the cholera became so frequent that one of their kings ordered the people to build upon the river itself, which, ' owing to greater cleanliness and better ventilation,' proved to be much more healthful. The houses are built upon bamboo rafts, which extend for several miles along the river, four or six deep, chained together and to the shore; and each raft is secured to a pole driven into the muddy bottom by rattan ropes, in such a manner as to allow of its rising and falling with the tide. It is said there are as many as twelve thousand of these floating dwellings and shops. Siamese houses are generally built of bamboo, covered in roofs and sides with *atap-*palm leaves, and are one storey in height. Those on the river front are mostly shops owned by Chinamen; they have two little peaked roofs and a small verandah, and one side is left open to display goods to those passing on the river. When a family dwelling in a floating house wish to move, they simply cast off the moorings and float with the tide up or down the river, as the case may be. There are said to be only two divisions in a Siamese house; of these one is occupied by males and the other by females. The floors of the houses which are built (raised upon piles) on the banks of the canals are reached by ladders, those on the river have small landing-places and steps on their rafts.

The existence of the Siamese, like that of the Burmese, may almost be said to be amphibious; they seem to pass more than half their lives in or on the water, and their chief food is the supply they get from it, fish. Everywhere we see canoes and boats, many of them propelled by women and little boys. 'Boats are the universal means of conveyance and communication. Except about the palaces of the kings, horses or carriages are never seen [1858], and the sedan of the Chinese appears unknown in Siam; but a boat is a necessary part of every person's household; to its dexterous management every child is trained; women and men are equally accustomed to the use of the oar, the paddle, and the rudder. From the most miserable skiff which seems scarcely large enough to hold a dog, to the magnificently adorned barge which is honoured with the presence of royalty, from the shabbiest canoe hewn out of the small trunk of a tree from the jungle up to the roofed and curtained, the carved and gilded bark of the nobles—every rank and condition has its boats plying in endless activity, night and day, on the surface of the Menam waters.'

For nearly half a mile both banks of the canal were lined with rice factories, owned, almost without an exception, by the Chinese; their business is to separate the rice kernel from its *paddy* husk and pack it for shipment. Then we came to the *Wat Sah Kāte* pagoda, situated in a vast enclosure, containing besides, after the usual arrangement, two or three temples, with huge gilt images of Budha within them, a large building for preaching, the dwellings of the priests, and many pavilions for the use of worshippers; but the grounds were in a very dilapidated condition. The King had recently turned 'adrift' all the priests, several hundreds of them, to earn an honest living by hard work instead of begging, and so the *wat*, or temple, was closed to the public. The pagoda is not completed, but still sufficient has been built to convey an idea of the original design. It was erected by a prince about fifty years ago, and is the largest edifice of the kind in the city. Built of brick, the form is that of a bell, with a circumference of about a thousand feet, and an altitude of about two hundred and fifty feet. The sides are covered with small niches (probably intended as the

TEMPLE AND PAGODAS AT BANKOK

receptacle of idols), and many narrow, sunken staircases lead to the summit; a large one on the outside winds around it to the top, which is a level place about fifty feet square, and upon which rests another pagoda, perhaps seventy-five feet in height. This one has passages through it, and in the centre there is a small brass image of Budha. From the summit of this huge pile of brick may be obtained a very fine view of the city of Bangkok and its surroundings; though this is hardly a correct statement, for you see very few of the dwelling-houses of the city; here and there a *wat*, or pagoda, the river with its shipping, the palace of the King, and a waving sea of cocoa-nut and betel-nut palms, is about all that distinctly appears. The general appearance of Bangkok is that of a large, primitive village, situated in and mostly concealed by a virgin forest of almost impenetrable density. On one side beyond the city limits were *paddy* fields, and on the other to the very horizon stretched the exuberant jungle.

On the bank of the river opposite the palace stands the most remarkable pagoda in Bangkok, called *Wat Cheng*. While being rowed thither I was much struck with the resemblance of the Siamese women to the men, their features being very similar, being dressed nearly alike, and both having the head shaved in the same manner; but upon close inspection it was usually seen that there were some distinguishing marks—that the women wore a narrow scarf around the shoulders, and allowed a lock of hair, some three inches in length, to hang down before the ear. Seen from the river, the floating houses, swiftly-passing boats, rafts and pagodas, and palaces together form a scene partaking more perhaps of the quaint and odd than of either the beautiful or grand. The *Wat Cheng* pagoda is bell-shaped, with a lofty, tapering steeple —a *prachadi*, sacred spire; the whole probably two hundred and fifty feet in height. It is built of brick and plastered on the outside, which is wrought into a grotesque and fantastic mosaic with Chinese cups, plates, and dishes of all sizes and colours, broken and whole, so set in the plaster as to form figures of elephants, monkeys, demons and griffins, flowers, fruits, vines and arabesques. In large niches upon the sides, at nearly half the distance to its top, are images of Budha riding on three elephants. The grounds of *Wat Cheng*, some twenty acres in extent, embrace— besides the priests' dwellings, temples, preaching-room, library, and halls—beautiful flower and fruit gardens, ponds, grottoes, belvederes, and stone statues (brought

WAT CHENG PAGODA, BANGKOK.

from China) of sages, giants, warriors, griffins, nondescripts, &c. In returning to the hotel we stopped at a floating booth where a theatrical entertainment was in progress. The dresses of the performers were rich, and the acting was much in the Chinese style, though there was perhaps not so much wanting, the voices being pitched to a more natural key. A great part of the dialogue was in verse; and the accompanying music was most primitive and droll, consisting simply of beating two bamboo sticks together. A band of three 'pieces' was also in attendance, and the music discoursed was of a lively character, and very much resembled some of the Scotch and Irish airs. The play was gross and obscene throughout, as is usually the case among eastern nations. The Siamese are alike fond of their national music and drama.

In company with the Consulate interpreter, 'Henry' — a good-natured, intelligent Siamese, who spoke English quite well — I visited other of the temples and pagodas of Bangkok. To the *Wat Sah Prah Tam*, situated without the city walls, we were admitted by the porter in charge, after paying a silver *tical* (about 60 cts.) At one extremity of this temple was a large gilded image of Budha, with a smaller one just in front, both sitting cross-legged, and being surrounded by many costly garments. The walls were painted in gaudy colours, with pictures of the annual or semi-annual religious visit of the King and Court to this *wat*. In these paintings the landscapes were fairly executed,

TEMPLE OF THE SLEEPING IDOL, BANGKOK.

though the colours were too deep and decided, the contrasts too great, the perspective often at fault; and the figures were stiff, and faces smiling, but devoid of any distinguishing character. This *wat* and all Siamese *wats* are lofty buildings of brick, with roofs rising in connected but decreasing tiers, and projecting over deep verandahs, which are supported by rows of massive square pillars, some of them sixty feet in height, and the whole is covered with white cement. The roofs are usually made of varicoloured tiles, and at the ridge-pole extremities are wooden ornaments very much the shape and size of a bullock's horn, which give an odd and fanciful but rather graceful finish to the buildings. The doors are large and covered with fine carving, gilt and black; the windows (or rather window shutters, for there is no glass), which are numerous, are also carved and sometimes ornamented with small pieces of coloured glass.

There are many temples belonging to the Chinese, which race is so largely represented in the population of Bangkok. The largest of these, called *Wat Conlayer Nemit*, contains a brass, cross-legged (sitting) Budha, about fifty feet in height and forty in width at the bent knees. The immense roof of this temple is as much as one hundred feet from the ground. A great heap of betel-nuts was stored in one, and two or three keepers or priests were living in another corner of the sacred edifice. There were two smaller *wats* within the same enclosure; the one contained a brass Budha sitting upon a rock, supported by a copper elephant on one side and a leaden monkey looking up with reverential eyes on the other. The other *wat* contained a large central image of Budha, and about a hundred smaller ones in different positions, before and around it; some were made of lead, some of brass, some of mixed metal, some of wood, and 'Henry,' the interpreter, tells me there were some there also of gold and silver, presented by the princes and nobles, but the priest in attendance could not be induced to point out their locality. The walls were covered with coloured illustrations of Siamese tradition, fable, and history.

Having pretty extensively traversed the city by water, one day some friends proposed a horse-back ride to the palace walls and back. We rode over a good, macadamised road, built by the late Supreme King, to the main entrance of the palace, where we saw a battalion of native troops exercising. Halting for a few moments, we observed that their drill and evolutions were performed with rapidity and exactness. Their uniform consisted of yellow coats and blue trousers, with white canvas caps (navy pattern); their feet were bare, and their weapons were muskets and swords of European design and manufacture. The palace walls, fifteen feet high by twelve in width, with a notched parapet, and the trees conceal most of the

BRASS IDOL IN TEMPLE: BANGKOK

buildings within, though we noticed some such lofty structures as a clock-tower, also some *wats*, pagodas, and 'sacred spires.' The native houses have been torn down and cleared away for some considerable distance around the walls, and it is intended that this space shall be neatly turfed or arranged in parks and flower gardens. At one corner of the palace enclosure we passed the royal (black) elephant stables—a dozen in number—the 'white' elephant being housed within the walls. The gates of the palace are built of simple teak wood, embossed with huge nails, but they are neither strong nor handsome.

Near this part of the city the late King has laid out several streets at right angles to each other, and built upon them compact blocks of two-storey brick houses, which are now rented by the Government (the King?) to the people. The present King has followed the example of his royal father in these civic improvements. He has built a good road around the city just within the walls, and also several blocks of houses next adjoining those erected by the late King. In several instances the intersection of two streets has been made or built into a circus, having a fountain or tower in the centre. And thus are some small transplanted shoots, taken from the great tree of western civilisation, with its wide-spreading branches of progressive thought and action, slowly but surely taking root in the receptive soil of Siam, once so vain and capricious. Having roads, the Siamese will next have ox-carts or carriages; indeed, some of the nobles have already imported the latter from Calcutta, and they may now occasionally be seen taking a drive, at the fashionable hour of the afternoon, sitting gravely upright, and as they roll along the dusty streets looking upon their friends and neighbours with a very perceptible sense of new-found importance, illustrative of deep culture and nice refinement. The Supreme King himself is also accustomed to take the air in a barouche drawn by six horses, with liveried postillions, and attended by gorgeous outriders and a mounted escort of the royal guard.

SUPREME KING OF SIAM IN HIS STATE ROBES

CHAPTER XII.

EXCURSION TO PECHABURI

To the kindness of the American Consul I was indebted for an introduction to the Private Secretary of the Second King and Secretary of the Foreign Office — a Mr. Chandler, formerly of Connecticut. This gentleman told me he came out to Siam twenty-eight years ago in the capacity of a missionary. He has lived here during the reign of three Siamese kings, and has witnessed the arrival and departure of several foreign missions, whose commercial leagues or treaties with Siam he has often been instrumental in furthering or negotiating. He has seen the country progress in legislation and commerce, until now nearly every western Power is represented by its consul resident at Bangkok, and Siam is fast becoming one of the most enlightened nations east of Calcutta. Several years ago Mr. C. gave up his missionary labours and entered the Government service, first as an interpreter, next as tutor to the King, and then as Secretary of the Foreign Office, which latter position he at present

retains. Mr. Chandler's family consists only of a wife—
a most worthy lady, who came from home with her
husband to assist him in his religious labours, and who
now employs her time in teaching about a dozen
Siamese boys the English language and rudiments of
education. From this excellent couple I received every
hospitality, and now, from afar, desire to tender them
my most heartfelt acknowledgments.

One day when relating to Mr. Chandler what I had
seen of interest in Bangkok, he said to me: 'Before
leaving Siam you should visit a large town about
100 miles south-west of here, called Pechaburi. It is
a sanitarium for both Europeans and natives, and the
King has built himself a palace there, also some
temples, some good roads and bridges. You go
there,' continued my friend, 'in a large barge, called
a "house" boat, rowed by six men, and in which you
eat and sleep, carry your books and papers, and at
your ease survey the country and people as you pass
along.' 'It would be a pleasant and interesting excursion surely,' I replied, ' and, not being pressed for
time, I will go. Perhaps the Consul's son would like
to take a rest from his official duties and make the
trip with me; I will ask him.'

Mr. Partridge, upon consultation, like the redoubtable Barkis, 'was willin;' and a large 'house' boat with five rooms, a cook, and table-boy having been engaged, we slipped away from the Consulate, rowed up the beautifully-lighted Menam — the Mother of Waters—and turned into the canal leading westward from about the centre of the city on the evening of the 7th of January. Our beds, with the ubiquitous mosquito nettings above them, had been placed in the comfortable cabin, our clothes and provisions packed away underneath its floor, and the cooking utensils, ready for use, were arranged in the stern quarter, back of the cabin. About nine o'clock on the following morning we stopped for breakfast and to rest our crew, who had rowed hard most of the night; and while we foreigners ate, the boatmen looked curiously on, and then in turn when they ate we gazed, no doubt, quite as curiously at them and their strange meal. Siamese food, at least that of the lower classes, consists principally of dried (often putrid) fish and rice, which are eaten in the form of curries, highly seasoned with pepper and spices. All classes in Siam use a sauce called *namphrik*, which differs from the Burmese fish condiment *ngapee*, in that a greater variety of articles are employed in its composition; it also mixes with rice like the Indian *chutnee*, though it approximates more in appearance and flavour to this paste than does the Burmese *ngapee*. The Siamese sauce is prepared, when all the desired ingredients are at hand, 'by bruising a quantity of red pepper in a mortar, to which are added *kapi* (paste of shrimps and prawns), black pepper, garlic, and onions. These being thoroughly mixed, a small quantity of brine and citron-juice is added. Ginger, tamarinds, and gourd seeds are also employed.' That the *namphrik* is 'one of the most appetite-exciting condiments' I know myself by experience; it is also, though very hot and 'high,' a savoury and toothsome addition to the ordinary curry of simple meat, rice, and gravy. People who are rich of course provide themselves with a variety of dainties. The Siamese eat from a common dish, with the fingers usually, though sometimes they use small spoons made of china or mother-of-pearl: water or tea is drunk with their meals, of which it is customary to have but two in the day—the breakfast at seven in the morning, and the dinner between the hours of five and six in the afternoon. Between meals, during the day, they chew the betel-nut, and smoke cigarettes made of native-grown tobacco, rolled in little slips of palm-leaf. The Siamese sometimes drink strong spirit in the form of arrack (made from boiled rice, molasses, and palm wine), though very rarely, and almost always secretly.

During the morning we crossed the Mahachen river, its banks thickly clad with verdure, and a canal which was straight and about thirty miles in length. The country was level, and at first only covered with rank grass; and we passed but few villages. But afterwards the banks of the canal were lined with bananas and *atap* palms, and beyond were market gardens and *paddy* fields. The capital is in great part supplied by the vegetables raised here; and the renters of the land and the labourers are almost all Chinese. In the afternoon we crossed another river—the Haichin—and late in the evening entered and rowed for a considerable distance down the Meklong—a large and deep river—and passed into another canal and anchored for the night. The banks of the Meklong seemed to be thickly settled, and the country in the distance was undulating and even hilly. A town called Meklong, near the mouth of this river, was the birthplace of the famous Siamese Twins. The face of the country improved as regards trees and vegetation as we went on, until we entered the Pechaburi river, which we were in and out of half a dozen times, while cutting off long and sinuous reaches by short cross-canals.

At three o'clock we arrived at Pechaburi, and having anchored at the outskirt of the town, sent our letters from the Consul at Bangkok to the Governor, requesting the use of a house, horses, &c., during our stay. The reply of the Governor, coming at last, allotted us a small brick house, furnished (?) with some bamboo mats, a table, and two chairs, upon the banks of the river: the lower storey or portion of the building had been set apart for, and evidently been recently used by, some domestic animals, such as sheep and dogs, and perhaps horses. In the evening we took a long walk through the bazaars and market along a macadamised street lined by substantial two-storey brick houses. The variety and quality of the native food exposed for sale in the market quite astonished both of us. The town of Pechaburi, built on both banks, and twenty miles from the mouth of a river bearing the same name, contains about twenty thousand inhabitants; it is about a hundred miles distant southwest from Bangkok, and is situated near the range of hills which divides the kingdom of Siam from the Tenasserim Provinces. Pechaburi is chiefly noted as a royal sanitarium. At the back of the town, on the summit of a beautiful hill, stands a large palace, built by the late Supreme King. On an adjoining hill are some pagodas and temples, and at the foot of the hill are some Budhist monasteries, where native youth are gratuitously educated, and near these is a cave filled with idols. There are some fine roads in and about Pechaburi, which were also built by the late King. On our return to the boat we met the Governor riding in a buggy, but he stopped, and we had some conversation with him through the interpreter. The Governor of Pechaburi was a young man, not intellectual or smart-looking; he was dressed in a European shirt and sun-hat (*topee*), with the native *panoung*, or cloth, which is worn around the waist and passed between the legs, striped socks, and patent-leather slippers. His servants laid abjectly upon the ground, with their feet behind them (in Burmese fashion), whenever they addressed His Excellency. In the buggy there was a finely-wrought gold *sroh*, or betel-box—an article in almost constant requisition by every Siamese nobleman.

Two missionaries of the American Presbyterian Board, with their families, live here, and they are the only foreigners in the town. Later in the evening we called upon the Rev. Mr. MacFarland; his *confrère*, who owns the adjoining house, was away on a leave of absence at the time. The reverend gentleman

—from Pennsylvania, U.S.—has lived twelve years in Siam, and has enjoyed very good health, notwithstanding the trying climate. He speaks the Siamese and Laos dialects perfectly, and thoroughly understands the people and their country after so long a residence. Mr. MacFarland told me he had made about twenty converts—that only one had relapsed into his old faith during his ministration. I remarked that I thought the Siamese seemed much more anxious to learn English than they were to acquire new religious tenets. He assented, but doubted the value of a general diffusion of the English language, notwithstanding there were no scientific, literary, or educational books as yet translated into the Siamese vernacular. He thought that the mission was too young to have expected greater successes—that the harvest truly was plenteous, but the labourers were few.

Perhaps the most interesting buildings in Pechaburi are those constituting the King's palace, which is situated upon a low hill near the town. His Majesty and some members of the Court are accustomed to spend part of every summer there. Riding across the plain to the foot of the hill, and there dismounting, we walk over a wide brick-paved path to the top, passing on the way many *salas*, or sheds open on the sides, and used for entertainments of various kinds, for quartering soldiers, &c. One of these sheds contained four or five mounted twelve-pounder cannon. The grounds were in a wretched state, being overgrown with weeds, but upon the annual visits of the King everything is put in good order. The path soon led us up steep staircases, with massive stone balustrades, and by several plain two-storey brick buildings used by His Majesty's friends and officers. Next we approached the private apartments of the King, with their wide, paved terraces and surrounding barracks. On the very summit of the hill, which is quite sharp, are three buildings—the royal audience hall, a temple, and an observatory. The audience hall is almost entirely without ornament. It is a long, low room about seventy-five feet in length by forty in width and twelve in height. The exterior walls are decorated between the windows, with a poor representation, carved in wood, of the flags of all nations existing upon the globe—evidently a recent addition to the building. The interior walls and ceilings are covered with a dingy-brown paper. At one end of the room is a semicircular throne, consisting of four stone steps, and painted upon the walls on either side are some excellent samples of Siamese art. The subjects are, of the one, the 'Reception of the French Ambassadors at Court,' and of the other 'Bonzes worshipping Gaudama.' The observatory is a round brick tower about thirty feet in height. From its top the country, as far as we could see, was a vast plain of *paddy*, broken here and there on every side by small, thickly wooded hills—luxuriant islets in a waveless sea of verdure—away to the north and west were low ranges of dark-blue mountains, and upon the south shone brightly, in the rays of the rising sun, the tranquil Gulf of Siam.

After a long ride we reached a large *wat*, near which, in the side of one of the hills, is a subterranean cavern, styled the 'Cave of Idols,' consisting of several small chambers connected by narrow passages. Light is admitted through one or two openings in its ceiling, though the greater part requires to be illuminated by torches. Judging from its material and structure, we thought the cave to be of volcanic origin. Its sides, within, are lined with rows of gilt Budhas, and at the end of one of the halls there is a huge reclining image of the same divinity. The trees about the mouth of the cave were filled with chattering and grinning monkeys. At sight of us they scampered from branch to branch and tree to tree, and then would sit still and

steadily observe us in a most amusing manner for as
much as an entire minute at a time. At the bottom
of the hill we inspected a temple in which was an
immense reclining Budha. This colossal image was
built of brick and *chunam* (lime), and covered with
thick gold-leaf; it was clothed with yellow (the
priestly colour) garments, and lay in the ordinary state
of repose, its head upon the right hand and resting on
a gaily ornamented pillow. I paced the length of this
idol, and made it to be 135 feet—its feet being seven
feet in width, ears ten feet in length, and other
members of like enormous proportions. The object
the priests have in view in building such monstrous
statues of Budha is to impress and awe the (common)
people, and, besides, the larger the idol the more merit
there will accrue to its makers.

A few miles from Pechaburi is a Laos village. It
consists of only about twenty huts. These are built
upon piles and made of bamboo, roofed with palm
leaves. Under the floors are stables for the domestic
animals and space for rubbish of all kinds. We entered the house of the chief magistrate of the village—
an old man, wearing nothing but a cotton *panoung*
(waist cloth). He cheerfully showed us his house,
which had but two rooms—a small one used as a

general sitting-room, and a large one intended for both kitchen and bed-chamber—and which was the home of a large family, whose relationships embraced three generations. Furniture there was none, excepting a few baskets and some large boxes. In the rear of the hut, but attached to it, was a large bin, made of bamboo and plaster, in which was stored rice (their 'staff of life,' or bread). The chief city of the Laos people in Northern Siam is Xiengmai, with about fifty thousand inhabitants. The Laos tribes have been many times at war with Siam, and have generally proved themselves to be no mean adversaries.

Pechaburi is a very pretty place, and it is justly popular with Europeans resident at Bangkok as a summer resort for a change of air or a little bit of rustication. We left it, very reluctantly, on the 11th, and reached Bangkok late on the following evening.

THE SECOND KING OF SIAM, IN STATE ROBES

CHAPTER XIII.

AUDIENCE WITH THE KING OF SIAM

It had been my earnest desire to obtain an audience with the Supreme King of Siam, but, as His Majesty was in Calcutta at the time of my visit, of course the wish could not be gratified; still, I could hardly esteem myself less fortunate in being granted, through the kind intervention of the American Consul, an audience with the Second King, H.M. Krom Prah Racha Wang Bowawn Bawara Sabtan Mongkon. Siam, I believe, is the only country in the world at the present day which is ruled by two kings. The position of the Second King is, however, not clearly understood. His office would hardly correspond with our Vice-President, nor is he exactly a co-ruler, nor the successor to the Supreme King; nevertheless his 'opinion and sanction are sought on important State policy, and his name is associated in treaties.' The late Sir John Bowring, a most excellent authority, says that 'the institution of a Second King is one of the peculiarities of the Siamese usages. He is not charged, as in the case of Japan [formerly], with the religious as distinguished from the civil functions of government, but exercises a species of secondary or reflected authority, the limits of which did not appear to me to be clearly defined. . . . He is said to dispose of one-third of the State revenue, and to have at his command an army of about 2,000 men. He is generally a brother or near relation of the King. . . . His palace is nearly of the same extent as that of the First King. . . . He is surrounded with the same royal insignia as the First King, though somewhat less ostentatiously displayed; and the same marks of honour and prostration are paid to his person. He has his ministers corresponding to those of the First King, and is supposed to take a more active part in the wars of the country than does the First King. It is usual to consult him on all important affairs of State. . . . He is expected to pay visits of ceremony to the First King,' &c. Thus it will be seen that the position of the Second King in the government of Siam is most peculiar and anomalous.

On the occasion of our visit His Majesty the Second King intended to have a parade of some of his household troops, and had invited the Austrian and

German Consuls to accompany us to the palace; Mr. Chandler, the Private Secretary, was also to be present, and act as marshal and interpreter. At three o'clock on the afternoon of the 15th inst. I repaired to the U.S. Consulate, and found General Partridge awaiting me, dressed in full military uniform, with an elegant sword dangling by his side. We then took boat— with the 'stars and stripes' proudly floating at the stern and the Siamese rowers in livery—to the house of Mr. Chandler, whom we found ready, in diplomatic dress, the brass buttons of his coat being stamped with the royal elephant of Siam, and together we walked to the palace gate, where we heard that the Austrian and German Consuls, with their secretaries, had preceded and were awaiting us in the royal reception hall. The guards presented arms as we entered the lofty gateway and walked upon a brick-laid path between what seemed to be the abodes of the Court servants and quarters for the troops. At the second gate (there are three walls about the palace) more guards saluted, and we passed across a small open square, surrounded by temples, *salas*, barracks, and dwellings, and were ushered into a large *wat*, which is now used as a waiting-room. Carpets had been spread upon the floor, and around a small table were sitting the German

Consul, Baron ———, a short gentleman in a captain's uniform (black, trimmed with red), wearing a faded order, and having a small glass cocked in one eye; and at his side the Austrian Consul, a Bangkok merchant, in tasty diplomatic dress, with white kid-gloves.

Soon an aide-de-camp entered, and announced that His Majesty was quite ready to receive us. We were directed across the square already mentioned, past a low shed, in which was a European fire-engine, buckets, axes, and other paraphernalia for extinguishing a conflagration; through another gateway, with more guards saluting; by the King's carriage-house, which we noticed contained several handsome Calcutta-built vehicles; and through a small but very pretty garden, laid out in Chinese style, to the palace, which consists of a number of small two-storey houses, built according to the rules (or rather vagaries) of Chinese architecture. Ascending a very narrow marble staircase, we were met at its top by the King himself, who cordially shook hands with us all, each being introduced in turn by Mr. Chandler. We were ushered into a small parlour, having in the centre a table, around which we seated ourselves in comfortable arm-chairs, the King with us. The walls of the room were hung with Chinese pictures, a chandelier for candles depended from the ceiling, a Brussels carpet lay upon the floor, a small book-rack stood in one corner, a Japanese lacquered *étui* in another, two guns with cloth covers in another, and two umbrellas in a stand at one side and a large gilt spittoon by the table completed the furniture of the room.

His Majesty is a fine-looking man, with a large and powerful though not corpulent body, and a large, shapely head, the perceptive and reflective faculties being about equally well developed; his hair is thin but black, eyes hazel-brown, teeth regular, but discoloured by the use of the betel-nut, his age about fifty. In conversation the King smiles pleasantly, and impresses one as a man of more than ordinary ability, energy, and tact. He was dressed very plainly, with no orders or insignia, wearing only a blue-black silk jacket with stand-up collar and steel buttons; a white linen vest, buttoning up close to the neck; a drab silk *panoung*, dropping as low as the knees; and a pair of cloth sandals, of peculiar construction, upon his otherwise bare feet. The King understands English pretty well, but is a little embarrassed in speaking that language with strangers. He is well acquainted with

English literature, and possesses also a tolerable knowledge of Western science, philosophy, and politics. His Majesty has been named after our great General and first President, for preceding half a dozen Siamese titles, is that of 'George Washington,' and the King previous to mounting the throne was generally known among the European residents of Bangkok as 'Prince George.'

Coffee and tea were brought in by three or four servants, who had been lying flat upon the floor of the verandah, and who crawled upon all fours into the room and, without lifting their eyes, placed the cups upon the table. And the King offered us from a magnificent open-work gold box cigars and cigarettes of Siamese manufacture; the latter, having wrappers made of the lotus flower, gave rise to a long conversation about the lotus, and also the *Victoria Regia* lily, &c. Then the talk was of birds of Paradise and pheasants; and then the King questioned me concerning the King of Ava and Mandalay. During our call His Majesty showed us some maps of Siam, drawn on a very large scale from recent Government surveys, and executed in a most beautiful manner, with the pen, by Siamese artists; the names of towns, mountains, and rivers were marked in Roman characters.

After this, the King intimating to Mr. Chandler that some of his troops were ready to perform their drill for our amusement, we adjourned to the square, and found there some matting spread upon the ground and a row of chairs for our convenience. His Majesty soon followed in a sedan chair, carried by eight bearers, with the royal umbrella suspended above his head, and preceded and followed by attendants bearing gilded spears. He requested us to be seated, and took a chair upon the right, facing us. Immediately an attendant brought a small table, and placing it by the King's side, put upon it a magnificent gold-embossed sword, a gold betel-box, cigar-box, and a tray with two small cups of perfumed liquor, and at the royal feet laid a large gold-plated spittoon. We seated ourselves in a line, the General occupying the place of honour, and the parade began at once.

There were two companies of troops, which marched in quick time from their barracks. The Second King has two thousand soldiers; but these were picked men (or rather boys, for such they were), who guard the palace and its royal occupants, and of whose proficiency in military tactics His Majesty is especially proud. They have had various instructors (drill-masters) at different times—French, English, and German; the orders which we heard were given in broken German. Their uniform of white duck is patterned after that worn by the British troops in India; they wear also (*mirabile dictu!*) shoes and socks. The companies, in turn, went through the manual of arms, and performed some skirmishing in remarkably good style; the musket drill was better than that of many of our so-called 'crack' regiments at home. After the

THE ROYAL GUARDS.

parade His Majesty's own brass band played for us. There were sixteen instrumentalists, led by a sergeant-major, a mere youngster seven or eight years old and three feet in height; indeed, none of the members of the band were more than twenty years of age; their uniform was the same as that worn by the guards. They played in remarkably good time and tune, first the 'Siamese National Hymn,' a rather pretty composition; and, second, a very familiar western waltz.

Afterwards another band of musicians, who were older, but had had less practice, were ordered out, and they rendered a piece of dance music tolerably well. We then took leave, shaking hands with the King, and returned through the same gateway we had entered, the guards being drawn up in line and saluting as we passed.

One morning at six o'clock, a few days afterwards I called, in company with General Partridge and Mr. Chandler, upon the Regent of Siam, our object being to obtain information concerning an overland route to Saigon, in Cochin China (an excursion proposed for myself), and to procure, if possible, letters of introduction from His Grace to the governors of the several provinces through which it would be necessary to journey. We were to meet the high Siamese official on board his steam yacht 'Rising Sun' (400 tons burden) according to appointment. Being upon the Menam at such an early hour of the morning, I was enabled to see the *bonzes* going their daily rounds to gather the alms by which they live. Each priest was seen sitting in a little canoe, having before him a large iron pot and one or two bowls, and thus paddling from house to house receiving contributions—nowhere does Budhism hold so pure and absolute a sway as in Siam—of rice, fish, vegetables, fruit, cakes, &c., which were dealt out to them from large brass urns, generally by women, the priests never returning thanks, but paddling away as if they had conferred a favour upon the charitable donors instead of the contrary. I noticed as many as a dozen *bonzes* waiting around one house in turn. It is considered a deed of merit to give alms to these priests, and daily at sunrise they go the rounds of the city. And it is said that no less than ten thousand of them are fed solely in this manner.

By Mr. Chandler I was presented to His Grace Chow Phya Sri Sury Wongse, the Regent. We were invited to take seats at a small table, covered with the usually-seen gold betel-boxes, spittoons, cigar-boxes, &c., His Grace sitting at its head. The Regent is a short, thick-set gentleman about sixty-five years of age; he was dressed in much the same manner as the Second King on the occasion of our recent audience with His Majesty. The Regent had an intellectual forehead and bright, intelligent eyes, but his mouth seemed to indicate a rather crabbed and petulant disposition, the latter perhaps caused by his old age and the anxieties of a busy and responsible life. He wears his hair in true Siamese fashion, viz. a tuft upon the crown of the head, the remainder being shaven about once a month at a certain stage of the moon. While conversing with us he smoked a small Chinese pipe, and often rose and walked about the deck in a very nervous, fidgety manner. Mr. Chandler showed His Grace my sapphire

THE REGENT OF SIAM

ring, remarking that it was presented by the present reigning King of Ava, Mounglon; whereupon His Grace asked me several questions (it should be remembered that Siam and Burma are old-time enemies)

about Mandalay, the capital, and among others 'if the
King went out much.' Upon my replying 'Never,' he
said (in *English*, the remainder of the conversation
being in Siamese), with a merry twinkle of the eye, 'He
'fraid they shoot him.' 'No, your Grace,' I replied, 'it
is not that; King Mounglon fears if he ventures beyond
his palace walls that upon his return he will very
likely find the gates closed and barred, and perhaps
hear that another sits upon the royal throne instead,' at
which answer he laughed heartily. The Regent's attendants were all of them girls, and very good-looking girls
they were too; they crept about the deck and noiselessly
executed any orders received from their 'august lord.'
Mr. Chandler asked His Grace the best and safest
route to the temples of Angkor, in eastern Siam, and he
replied, 'That by Kabin, through the forests, about
east:' the other route being by sea down the gulf
to Tang Yai, and then crossing overland to the ruins.
The Regent told us that the Governor of Kabin, having
been in town on official business, had left only that
very morning to return to his province; that he would
obtain for us a bullock-cart, horses, &c., upon our
arrival there; and that he himself would request the
Minister of Foreign Affairs, or his representative, to
furnish us with the much-desired and very necessary

AUDIENCE WITH THE KING OF SIAM   157

letters of introduction and passports, for use on our unusual and somewhat perilous excursion. Touching the tips of His Grace's fingers, we then withdrew, having heartily but respectfully thanked him for the honour of the interview and its favouring results.

The prominent position in the government of Siam

MINISTER OF FOREIGN AFFAIRS

which Chow Phya Sri Sury Wongse has occupied before the world for the past twenty years or more prompts me to add something further concerning this rare and admirable statesman. Ever since Sir John Bowring's visit in 1855 the Regent has been 'the real ruler of Siam;' his ability and influence are most remarkable and his successes undoubted. At the time of the negotiation of the treaty of friendship and commerce between H.B.M. and the Kings of Siam the Regent was *Phra Kalahom*, or Prime Minister (his son holds the office at present), and was one of the four commissioners appointed by the Supreme King to discuss and decide upon that treaty on the part of the Siamese Government.

Sir John Bowring thus had much intercourse with His Grace, and in his 'Personal Journal' has written a just estimate of his many excellent qualities. Says Sir John in one place, 'It is quite a novelty to hear a minister abuse the administration of which he is the head. He confirms his statements by facts; he mentioned instances of bribery and extortion: in a word, his language is of the most high-minded patriotism.' And in another place he writes, 'The personal character of the Prime Minister is to me an object of much admiration. He is the most distinguished man of the greatest family in the empire. . . . He has again and again told me that if my policy is to save the people from oppression and the country from monopoly he shall labour with me, and if I succeed my name will be blest to all ages. He unveils abuses to me without disguise, and often with vehement eloquence. If he prove true to his profession [which he most honourably did] he is one of the noblest and most enlightened patriots the Oriental world has ever seen. To him Siam owes her fleet of merchant ships.'

The sequel has proved that this rather florid praise was not exaggerated, and that the nobility of His Grace's nature has not been over-estimated. During the absence of the Supreme King in Singapore, Calcutta, and British India, and notwithstanding the Second King still remained at Bangkok, the vacillating helm of the 'ship of state,' with all its 'tearful interests,' was readily and confidently entrusted for the time to His Grace Chow Phya Sri Sury Wongse, Regent of Siam.

CHAPTER XIV.

A DAY IN THE PALACE

One day of my stay at Bangkok was pleasantly spent within the palace walls, with Mr. Chandler as my obliging cicerone. We went first to see the so-called 'white' elephants. These are kept, fastened to stout posts, in large sheds, and covered with gilt canopies, in the same manner as the one I saw at Mandalay, which belonged to the King of Ava. The first animal whose stable we entered was quite small, and possessed few of the peculiar characteristics of a 'dark-cream albino,' excepting perhaps the eyes. The keeper fed him with bananas, and caused him to make a salaam (a profound salutation or bow) by raising his proboscis to his forehead for a moment and then gracefully lowering it to the ground. In another shed we saw a larger and also whiter elephant, its body having the peculiar flesh-coloured appearance termed 'white.' Here there was, besides, a white monkey—'white animals are the favourite abodes of transmigrating souls'—kept to ward off bad spirits, as the attendant informed us.

Sir John Bowring—and he is about the only person who has written at length on this subject—in a very interesting 'Chapter on Elephants,' tells us that the Budhists have a special reverence for white quadrupeds; that he has himself seen a white monkey honoured with special attention. Also, that white elephants have been the cause of many a war, and their possession more an object of envy than the conquest of territory or the transitory glories of the battlefield. In the money market a white elephant is almost beyond price. Ten thousand sovereigns ($50,000) would hardly represent its pecuniary value; a hair from its tail is worth a Jew's ransom. 'It was my good fortune,' he says, 'to present [in 1855] to the First King of Siam (the Siamese have two kings exercising supreme authority) presents with which I had been charged by my royal mistress. I received many presents in return; but the monarch placed in my hand a golden box, locked with a golden key, and he informed me the box contained a gift far more valuable than all the rest, and that was a few hairs of the white elephant. And perhaps it may be well to state why the white elephant is so specially reverenced.

'Because it is believed that Budha, the divine

emanation from the Deity, must necessarily, in his multitudinous metamorphoses or transmissions through all existences, and through millions of aeons, delight to abide for some time in that grand incarnation of purity which is represented by the white elephant. While the *bonzes* teach that there is no spot in the heavens above, or the earth below, or the waters under the earth, which is not visited in the peregrinations of the divinity—whose every stage or step is towards purification—they hold that his tarrying may be longer in the white elephant than in any other abode, and that in the possession of the sacred creature they may possess the presence of Budha himself. It is known that the Cingalese have been kept in subjection by the belief that their rulers have a tooth of Budha in the temple of Kandy, and that on various tracts of the East impressions of the foot of Budha are reverenced, and are the objects of weary pilgrimages to places which can only be reached with difficulty; but with the white elephant some vague notions of a vital Budha are associated, and there can be no doubt that the marvellous sagacity of the creature has served to strengthen their religious prejudices. Siamese are known to whisper their secrets into an elephant's ear, and to ask a solution of their perplexities by some sign or movement. And most assuredly there is more sense and reason in the worship of an intelligent beast than in that of stocks and stones, the work of men's hands.

'And yet,' continues Sir John, 'after all the white elephant is not *white*, nor anything like it. It is of a coffee colour; not of unburnt, but of burnt coffee—dull brownish yellow or yellowish brown—white only by contrast with his darker brother. The last which reached Bangkok was caught in the woods. The King and Court went a long way out into the country to meet him, and he was conducted with a grand procession, much pomp, and music, and flying banners, to the capital. There a grand mansion awaited him, and several of the leading nobility were appointed his custodians. The walls were painted to represent forests, no doubt to remind him of his native haunts, and to console him in his absence from them. All his wants were sedulously provided for, and in his "walks abroad," when "many men he saw," he was escorted by music and caparisoned by costly vestments. His grandest and farthest promenades were to bathe in the river, when other elephants were in attendance, honoured by being made auxiliaries to his grandeur. Now and then the two sovereigns sought his presence,

but I did not learn that his dignity condescended to
oblige them with any special notice. But he wanted
no addition to his dignity. Everything associated with
majesty and rank bore his image. A white elephant is
the badge of distinction. The royal flags and seals,
medals and moneys—on all sides the white elephant is
the national emblem, as the cross among Christians or
the crescent among Turks; and the Siamese are prouder
of it than Americans, Russians, Germans, or French
are of their eagles, or Spaniards of the golden fleece.
The Bourbon *Oriflamme*, the British Union Jack, show
but faintly in the presence of the white elephant.'

Thus it will be seen that in Siam the 'white' elephant,
as in the kingdom of Ava, is a grave and important appendage of state, and that the King of Siam lays quite
as just claim to the coveted and pompous titles of
' Lord of the Celestial Elephant ' and ' Master of Many
White Elephants ' as does His Majesty of Ava.

In the arsenal of artillery were some enormous brass
cannon, said to have been made under the direction of
the Portuguese. One of them was full twenty feet
in length, mounted on a very clumsy wooden carriage;
another must have had a bore of eighteen inches in
diameter; another was engraved with the date 1627
and a Latin inscription. A plain two-storey building

TEMPLE OF THE EMERALD IDOL.

within the second wall had a sign over its door which read ‘Coining Manufacture’—some of the late King's droll English. We were shown through this establishment—the Royal Mint. The machinery is of English make, though none but Siamese workmen are employed. At the time of our visit the Mint was coining silver *ticals* (worth about 60 cts.) The courts of justice are simply large sheds with matted floors, like those in Mandalay. We could not obtain admittance to the Audience Hall; it is a large, fantastic-shaped building, with a lofty spire from its centre.

The *Wat Phran Kean*, or Temple of the Emerald Idol, is the finest of its class in Siam. The model is similar to the others, but the workmanship, both exteriorly and interiorly, is of a much higher order. The walls are covered with admirably executed paintings; the floor is laid over with brass bricks. The altar, built in the shape of a pyramid, about sixty feet high, is surmounted by the ‘Emerald Idol’—an image twelve inches in height and eight in width. ‘Into the virgin gold of which its hair and collar is composed,’ says a recent observer, ‘must have been stirred, while the metal was yet molten, crystals, topazes, sapphires, rubies, onyxes, amethysts, and diamonds—the stones crude and rudely cut, and blended in such proportions as might enhance to the utmost imaginable limit the beauty and the cost of the admired effigy.' On the altar there are many large images covered with pure gold, whose robes are ornamented with genuine precious stones; also some *lusus naturæ*, as extraordinarily formed tusks of the elephant and rhinoceros, beautifully carved marble statues, clocks, golden altar-utensils, and garments which belonged to the late King. The reigning monarch worships in this temple, and here also the nobles take the oath of allegiance. On either side of the principal entrance stand two life-size marble statues, whose history I could not learn, of Peter, 'the Apostle of Jesus Christ,' and of Ceres, the Roman goddess of agriculture. Near this *wat* is a small pagoda which, in an enormous pyramidal cabinet of ebony and mother-of-pearl, contains the Budhist sacred books. A carpet made of silver wire lies upon the floor. Adjoining this is a large pagoda which has been ten years in building, and has already cost over $200,000; and two years more will be necessary for its completion. The interior side of the wall which surrounds the Temple of the Emerald Idol is covered with gorgeous paintings of old Siamese fables and superstitions.

The palace where the Supreme King resides consists

of a large number of odd-looking houses crowded
together within the third wall. Very many buildings
could not be shown us because of the absence of the
King, and some others because they were undergoing
repairs at that time. An absurd custom prevails,
which requires that at the close of each reign all the
temples and most of the palace buildings shall be torn
down and new ones erected in their places, and if the
buildings themselves are not removed, at least their
ornaments and other accessories are carried away. We
next visited the temple *Wat Poh*, outside the palace
walls, in which is a 'reclining' Budha, 145 feet in
length, and 65 in height at the shoulders. It is built
of brick and *chunam*, thickly covered with leaf gold.
The soles of the feet, which are sixteen feet in length,
are covered with the mystic symbols peculiar to a
Budha, inlaid with mother-of-pearl, and finished with
gold-leaf.

The proposed overland excursion to the ruins at
Angkor was fast taking shape, and for four or five days
I was busily engaged in making the necessary preparations. I had invited the Rev. Mr. MacFarland, of
Pechaburi, and General Partridge to accompany me,
and to my delight both had accepted. We thought a
month only would be requisite to accomplish the entire

journey to Angkor and the return to Bangkok. I
proposed to go on alone to Panompin, the capital of
Cambodia, and thence down the great Makong river
to Saigon, in Cochin China; but the official duties of
both my companions would compel them, however
unwillingly, to return direct to Bangkok. First, it was
necessary to provide 'house' boats for the canal and
river travel, in which we hoped to accomplish one-
third of the distance; and these the General obtained,
together with interpreters, boatmen, and servants. He
secured as cook a strong and tough Chinaman named
'Deng,' who spoke English pretty well, and who was
one of the 'boys' whom M. Henri Mouhot, the French
naturalist, took with him up to Louang Prabang, a
town in north-eastern Siam; and who, with another
'boy,' buried there the brave traveller (who died of
the terrible fever, 1861), and returning, brought his
journal and letters to Bangkok. In his book of
'Travels in India, China, Cambodia, and Laos' M.
Mouhot tells some amusing stories about the character
and morals of this 'Deng;' one of these relates that
his attendant had a little defeat. 'He now and then
takes a drop too much, and I have found him sucking,
through a bamboo cane, the spirit of wine from one of
the bottles in which I preserve my reptiles, or laying

under contribution the cognac presented to me by my friend Malherbes [a merchant at Bangkok]. A few days ago he was seized with this devouring thirst, and profiting by my absence for only a few minutes, he opened my chest and hastily laid hands on the first bottle which presented itself, great part of the contents of which he swallowed at one gulp. I came back just as he was wiping his mouth with his shirt sleeve, and it would be impossible to describe his contortions and grimaces as he screamed out that he was poisoned. He had had the bad luck to get hold of my bottle of ink; his face was smeared with it, and his shirt was pretty well sprinkled. It was a famous lesson for him, and I think it will be some time before he tries my stores again.' But 'Deng' was a capital cook, M. Mouhot tells us, and so we expected great things of him; and we were not afterwards in any way disappointed, for he proved throughout one of our most faithful, hard-working, and obliging servants.

A part of my duty was to select and purchase the food supplies—liquors and provisions in bottles and tins; ale, brandy, sherry, and claret; meats, vegetables, biscuits, soups, condiments, &c.; and potatoes, rice, onions, hams, coffee and tea in bulk. We intended to rely principally upon these, though we also proposed to eke out our preserved, condensed, and desiccated victuals with the produce of the country through which we would journey, viz. rice, fish, poultry, eggs, and various fruits. I wasted much time in endeavouring to obtain a Cambodian interpreter, one speaking English, or even Siamese, who was willing to go with us, but met with no success. However, Mr. MacFarland's servant was a Cambodian by birth, and, though he had lived nearly all his life in Siam, still remembered sufficient of his native tongue to be of considerable service to us. We took an assortment of medicines, especially a liberal supply of *quinine*, three grains of which we were recommended to take every morning in our coffee by Dr. Hutchinson. Each one had his mattress, blankets, and mosquito netting, though all carried as little personal baggage as consisted with comfort and health. The offensive and defensive (especially) weapons of the party comprehended two revolvers and two or three large bowie-knives. We also carried a few scientific instruments and writing and drawing materials, maps of the country, a selection of books and old magazines, and I packed in my waterproof bag besides a few presents for the King of Cambodia, Governor of Siamrap, and some other great men. Money was carried in several small packages—

silver and copper coins—though our letters were quite
adequate to secure for us every hospitality and attention. These letters were simply official orders from the
Siamese Minister of Foreign Affairs to the governors
of the provinces through which it would be necessary
for us to pass: of one of these, written in the vernacular idiom, with the great seal of the Foreign Office
attached, I am able to give a translation, *verbatim et
literatim*, prepared for me by ' Henry,' the Consulate
interpreter. The passports were granted by the
Siamese Government on application of General F. W.
Partridge, as United States Consul. One reads:—

'Chow Phraya Pootarupai-metaya-pitayasai-mahattri-
nayoh-siamdilor-maha Senabodi, the Samuha-nayok; To
Phraya Utaimontri Sri-suraraj-bodintr-narintr Mataya
Mahaprichi-songkram, Governor of the Province of
Phra-Prachinburi, Phra Palat, the Lieutenant-Governor,
and the Provincial Officers of the province and dependencies:

'Phraya Pepat Hosa, the proper officer of the Foreign
Department, has presented the original letter of General
F. W. Partridge, U.S. Consul, stating that he, the said
Consul, is going on a tour to see the province of
Nakon Siamrap, on the north of the lake Talesap, on
the borders of Cambodia. General——, with those who

accompany him, are Americans, three in number, one interpreter, six Siamese, and one Chinese, in all *eleven persons*. —— and company will go by land from Pachim to Siamrap. Should —— and those who accompany him arrive at Pachim, let the Governor, the Lieutenant-Governor, and the Provincial Officers receive them and make such provision for their wants as becomes their rank. If when —— and his company go on to the province of Siamrap they are in want of provisions of any kind, let the Governor, the Lieutenant-Governor, and the Provincial Officers of Pachim and its dependencies provide for them, and give in a becoming manner. Also, provide for them elephants, carts, oxen, and buffaloes to take them on their way thither through the villages to the province and town of Siamrap in a manner becoming their honourable rank, and avoid complaint from the foreigners.

'Given on Thursday, the 8th day of the waxing moon, the 3rd month, year of the goat, 3rd of the decade, and 3rd year of the present reign; corresponding to the 18th of January, 1872.'

(Great Seal of the Foreign Office)

This *order*—a fine example of Siamese composition and usage—simply as a 'state paper' is quite worthy of being filed for preservation with the archives of our department at Washington. At any rate, to it principally we were indebted for the success of our expedition. In Indo-China, and in fact most countries of the East, the nations humbly reverence and honour rank and authority and its enjoinments; and they will readily find ways and means of complying with a governmental order when the demands and bribes or threats of an unknown, unrecommended, private traveller would avail nothing. Upon the governors of provinces remote from the metropolis and the ruling monarch we were dependent for our means of transportation—elephants, horses, buffaloes, carts, and servants—and everywhere on our journey, when the passport was produced, we were received with distinguished courtesy and consideration. And for such condescending favour and aid on the part of the Siamese Government it is only permitted me here to return my most respectful thanks to the leading authorities—to His Grace the Regent and the Minister of Foreign Affairs, and also to their subordinate officers, the governors of the provinces in eastern Siam—for the very hospitable manner in which they complied with their instructions from the distant capital.

But I am anticipating, for we are only now starting on our journey. Everything is ready, however, and so, on the evening of the 25th of January, 1872, we are at last off. There are three boats. In the first— a four-oar—voyages the General and his servant; next follows a six-oar, with the missionary and myself; and last goes a four-oar, containing our interpreter, my 'boy,' 'Deng' the Chinese cook, and the greater part of the provisions and baggage.

The great floating city, bathed in the pale moonlight, and at the same time illumined with ten thousand coloured lanterns, presents a strange, weird appearance as our boats swing away from the Consulate wharf, with their prows headed up the whirling Menam; the native boatmen break out in wild, whimsical, cadenced songs, keeping time to the regular, almost noiseless dip of their oars; as we sail along we hear the pariah dogs growling over their midnight prey, and we distinguish also a few strains, a trifle more melodious, of the monotonous music of a Chinese theatrical booth; and thus standing upon deck, with the flag of our so far away country floating over us, we wave a hasty adieu to Bangkok—the eastern Venice—and our many kind friends, and turning away, enter a narrow canal leading directly to the east—towards the very heart of Siam.

CHAPTER XV.

ACROSS SOUTHERN SIAM

THE BOATS were anchored about midnight, and in the spacious cabins we slept soundly until morning. With daylight we saw the canal was lined with bamboo huts, and that passing us were many boats on their way to Bangkok with market stuffs. In the middle of the day we stopped for an hour to allow the men rest and time for eating their fish and rice. The canal continued very narrow during the remainder of the day; its sides were covered with a thin strip of cocoa palms and bamboos, but the country beyond was a vast plain of rank jungle grass, with an occasional hut in sight, or a small village of a dozen or more dwellings, and always a cock-pit, licensed by, and a source of great revenue to, the Government. The huts were very dilapidated. A rule with the Siamese is never to repair a building, but to live in it until it almost falls upon their heads. The people appeared poor, and were certainly shockingly dirty. The mosquitoes proved very troublesome, becoming towards evening almost unbearable. We noticed that all the natives slept within curtains, and that the huge buffalo-cows were coralled in small swampy enclosures, in which they wallowed, covering themselves with mud and water as a protection against the stinging pests. At night we entered the nettings we were so careful not to leave behind, but no such thing as 'balmy sleep' could be obtained; there seemed to be quite as many mosquitoes within as without the curtains. They made a buzzing as of a thousand bees; the air was literally thick and heavy with them. The only respite we had from their attacks was when completely enveloped in our blankets; but this was simply 'from the frying-pan into the fire,' for the action nearly suffocated us. In the morning the General said he counted fifty of the merciless insects which were hanging on the *inner* side of his curtains, in a semi-torpid state, after the night's sanguinary foray; and my face was so red and swollen as scarcely to be recognisable by my companions.

On the morning of the second day from Bangkok we enter the Bang pa Kong river, which we propose to ascend about fifty miles to Pachim, the residence of a governor; and then, if possible, we shall go on by water to Kabin, thirty or forty miles farther. In an old *wat* where we breakfasted, thrown over a small image of Budha, was a piece of yellow cloth, about a foot in length and two inches in width, upon which was written in Siamese characters, 'This cloth I, Nang Yai, send to my aunt Sim; if anybody steals it, may he go to hell.' From which we understood that the cloth was consecrated to the memory of Nang's transmigrating aunt, and that he entertained pretty strong and precise feelings towards the person who should purloin the hallowed offering. The Bang pa Kong river is three or four hundred feet in width, deep, with strong tides and a very tortuous course; we did not pass a straight reach as much as an eighth of a mile in length. In the afternoon we observed an alligator about eight feet long, with open, cavernous mouth and sleepy, half-closed eyes, lying in the tall grass on the bank, enjoying the bright rays of the sun.

Arrived at Pachim, the Governor sent us an invitation to pass the night in a house which he had prepared for our reception (we had sent a messenger ahead to herald our approach), but we preferred sleeping on board the boats. The Governor's house we saw on the following morning. It is a large bamboo building, raised upon piles, and in the long room, having one side open, His Excellency received our party. Before us stood an old gentleman of short stature, intelligent and amiable countenance, with grey hair, and teeth much blackened by use of the betel. His dress was a silk coat and buff cloth waistcoat, with a simple *panoung*, and bare legs and feet; he wore besides a pair of immense spectacles. The room made a rather primitive 'audience chamber,' containing as it did only a small sofa, beyond which were some emblems of authority—large umbrellas, a bamboo mat, chandeliers hanging from the beams, and two paroquets with rich plumage in cages at either end; and there were also two clocks, both of which insisted upon indicating that the hour (at seven in the morning) was half-past one. Lying upon their hips, prostrate upon the floor, were a dozen or more officers and attendants. We conversed about half an hour with the Governor, through the missionary as interpreter. He promised to obtain three ponies for us, and four bullock-carts for our servants and baggage, and at taking leave he sent with us a present of meat and fish, asking what other provisions we were desirous of receiving. The Governor will send orders in advance to the sub-governors of the provinces between Pachim and Siamrap, who will have provisions and conveyance waiting, so that in future we may not be delayed.

The town of Pachim lies upon level ground on the north bank of the Bang pa Kong river, and contains, scattered over a large extent of country, some two or three thousand inhabitants. Anchored before the town were about fifty boats, some of them of large size, and owned by Chinamen; and back of the town the Government authorities were building a citadel and palace, the brick walls of which are to be six feet in breadth, and are to enclose a section of land about eight acres in extent. A saw-mill and brick-yard are in operation, preparing the materials of construction; we visited the latter. The work is mostly done by women. The bricks are made of clay and *paddy* husks, and are burnt: they sell for $2.40 a thousand, delivered in Bangkok. At the entrance of the new citadel we saw a remarkable natural gateway, formed by two trees (the *poh* species, the sacred tree of the Siamese, being that under which Budha is said to have expired when he left this world), about two feet in diameter at their bases, joining and growing together in the form of a perfect arch twenty feet from the ground, and towering up in a single trunk thirty feet higher, and spreading out in grand masses of bright green foliage. It seemed that formerly the gate of an old stockade stood there, which compelled the trees to either die or unite, and, owing to the fertility of the soil and their inherent vigour, they chose the latter, and so are now living united, like the Siamese twins. Near here was also another wonder—a *lusus naturæ* —two *poh* trees growing together, with a tamarind between them, and a *poh* tree, another tamarind, and a lofty and healthy toddy-palm tree standing interlaced in one cluster or group. We had an opportunity also to witness the native method of grinding *paddy*— hulling the grain—in a low bamboo shed. The mill consisted of two parts, of course, but, instead of the usual coarse stones, they were made of thin slabs of hard wood embedded in mud and surrounded by wicker-work. The motive power was a man and a woman, who worked this primitive machine by means of a long pole and a cross-piece of bamboo at one end, with the other fastened in a loose socket to the upper mill-stone (or rather mud and wood basket), it being the same principle as that applied to our grindstone. In the morning there came as a present from the Governor two kinds of dried fish, some eggs, oranges, and cocoa-nuts, and in the evening a dozen of fowls.

We arose at daylight on the 29th of January, removed our baggage from the boats, and sent them back to Bangkok, as from this point we were to travel by land. We retained of the servants the Chinese cook, Chinese butler or table-boy, and two Siamese 'boys'—personal attendants. Our horses and carts and bullocks—three of the former and eight of the latter—with their grooms and drivers, came about noon. The horses, or rather ponies, were so small and thin that we greatly feared their ability to bear us. The General had brought his own saddle and bridle from the Consulate, but the missionary and myself were to use native seats and head-stalls. The Siamese simply ride upon a cushion placed upon the horse's back, and held in position by the rider's knees and legs, without stirrups, and with a most primitive bridle, made usually of coarse twine. Natives on a journey are accustomed to alternately run at full speed and walk their horses, until the little beasts, warmed into a profuse white lather, almost drop from fatigue. The bullocks are black, very large and powerful; they are driven, with a line passed through the nostrils, as we direct horses. Most singular in appearance are the native carts. The body is built of a light but strong wood, the sides being of bamboo; it is usually about six feet in length, one or two feet in width at the bottom, and thrice as much at its top, which is a bamboo roof, projecting far beyond the body of the cart at the front end, where sits the driver, thus protected from the sun. The wheels are of solid wood, and about five feet in diameter; they turn upon small wooden axles. The Governor sent us a final present of sugar, cucumbers, and fried cakes, and nearly the entire town assembled to see us depart.

The road at first led over an even plain, for the most part covered with coarse grass, and in the distance were forests and a low range of blue mountains. Some *paddy* was cultivated by the roadside, but few dwellings, however, were seen. We on horseback travelled at the rate of three miles an hour, and the carts followed at about a mile per hour less. Having crossed the Bang pa Kong river, we shortly afterwards entered the village of Chantakan, distant fifteen miles from Pachim, and of about the same size—and were escorted by some of the people with torches to the residence of the Deputy-Governor. Instructions from the Governor of Pachim had preceded us, and this official had prepared for our use two newly built *salas*, where, after we were comfortably settled, he sent us a ready-cooked (Siamese) dinner. As our provisions had not yet arrived, we were glad as well as curious to partake of the native food. It was served upon three little wooden stands, half a dozen bowls upon each; there was neither knife, fork, nor spoon: Siamese eat with their fingers, and so did we. There was set before us fish cooked in five different styles, boiled rice, salad, and condiments, including, of course, *namphrik*, which, however, was made in a new way, mixed with fish oil and some other articles not very inviting to American palates; water for drinking was brought in large brass bowls. Before we had quite finished the repast three spoons were brought us—one of iron, another of porcelain, and another of mother-of-pearl, the latter being a clear, silvery shell, and handsomely cut. I induced its owner to part with it for a lead pencil and two or three sheets of note-paper.

We were off at daylight in the morning, and now travelled over a good but very dusty road—dusty at that particular time of year, and very preferable to the floods of water, which bring fevers and breed mosquitoes—and halted at noon, having accomplished about twelve miles. There were a goodly number of tall trees to be seen this day; especially interesting was a species from which the natives obtain a lubricating oil. Great fields of *paddy* stalks lay near the road; a little farther off was the dense forest, and a range of hills, just discernible, ran away to the northward. We saw the prairie-grass and woods burning in many places, and everywhere there were blackened and charred remains of recent fires, which the natives say are accidentally started or produced, perhaps by a match or a discarded cigar stump. They burn for months at a time, sometimes quietly simmering at the foot of an old tree, from which a sudden strong wind will scatter sparks into some dry vegetable matter, which of course will at once blaze up, and so the fire will spread and travel over immense districts of country. The villages we passed were all small—six or a dozen houses—with long distances between them; everything about the dwellings and people betokened great and general poverty; still the latter seemed nearly as happy and contented as they were dirty and curious.

Kabin we found to be a Laos town of about a thousand inhabitants. The Governor was absent when we arrived, but a subordinate made us comfortable in the public *sala*, while notice was sent to His Excellency of the arrival of the 'farangs' (foreigners). Our room was enclosed by fastening straw matting along its sides; water for bathing purposes was brought in large jars; then appeared servants bringing torches, fowls, eggs, and rice; and soon afterwards a dinner, served in true native style, consisting of ten little tables or stands, which held altogether some forty dishes of food. This latter civility we declined, and with the officer's permission gave the dinner to our servants: there was sufficient for all, and they exceedingly enjoyed what was to them, we doubted not, a most royal feast. In the evening the Governor called, an 'oldish' gentleman, with a pleasing face and engaging manners, dressed in a blue silk *panoung* and red and grey silk jacket, his head and feet being of course bare. He answered the missionary's questions and also our own so quickly and decidedly as to prove a most thorough acquaintance with his special province. He told us that the gold mine near there, worked entirely by Siamese, was paying pretty well at the time; and he showed us some of the gold, which had been manufactured into little filigree workboxes, for holding tobacco. Their workmanship was rude, but the gold is said to be the most ductile in the world; its colour is a dark, dull yellow, and it appears very soft. We informed the Governor that we wished to proceed on our journey at daylight, and he promised that we should have ponies and bullock-carts and that he would give us a letter to another Governor at the next town, some twenty-five miles distant. We were not expected to make any return or present to the servants we employed on the road; still we thought it right to award them something when faithful, and so we paid for the use of our animals and their drivers and attendants at the rate of half a *tical* each per diem. We entered this day upon the 'grand military road' built by the Siamese some thirty-five or forty years since for the easier transport of troops to the remote districts of their kingdom—parts of Cambodia and Cochin China, then recently annexed. The road was in such excellent condition, the General remarked, that over it might easily be drawn the heaviest artillery.

The Siamese have quite as vague and amusing impressions of distance as the Hindoos. We asked a traveller whom we met on the road a few days ago how far it was to the nearest well,' and received for reply, 'About as far as a dog can bark' (i.e. one could hear the animal). And again this morning we heard another ludicrous expression of distance; a town was 'as far as a cock could crow,' and we found it to be nearly half a mile—rather a far-fetched crow. In India once, when travelling on horseback in the Himalayas near the borders of Tibet, I chanced to pass eight several Hindoos on the road, and enquiring of each the distance to a particular town, no two answered me with the same number of *koss*, or miles (about two English), or else sometimes, when asking a similar question, I would receive for reply, 'Just a little before you' (*Tora aye hai*), or else, 'Go straight forwards' (*Seedha aye chule jas*), whether my destination was one or twenty miles distant, or there were a dozen turns or intersecting ways.

We next entered a region of very dense forest, through which the road was evenly cut, the branches of the trees joining just above our heads and making a complete shade. Some trees which we saw were over 200 feet in height and three feet in diameter; they were very straight, and did not branch until far above the ground. It is, however, not the best time of year to see the forests in their virgin splendour—the rainy season favours vegetation more—the trees now have rather too scanty foliage, too many ugly dead limbs, too many leaves, half green and half yellow. Tigers (wild), elephants, and other ferocious animals abound hereabouts, and our guides told us it would not be safe to travel at night; even during the day we carried loaded revolvers, and each of our 'boys' had large knives or two-edged daggers attached to cords and worn around their necks. On the march we distinguished the tracks of elephants and panthers, and at night listened to the howls of jackals prowling around our camp. The screams of monkeys, though we did not often see the wary little animals, the notes of peacocks, quails, parrots, and many unknown birds were also heard. One day, as we were quietly jogging along, we observed two immense birds standing together upon the grassy plain; they appeared to be of the adjutant species, with a long bill, black neck, broad white stripe round the body, black tail, and very long red legs, and were about four feet in height. As we journeyed on we also saw great turkey-buzzards, and occasionally a herd of red deer. It is customary with the natives to ensnare the latter by driving them into narrow enclosures, in which strong nets have been spread. It was our practice to walk as much as eight miles every day, the remainder being accomplished on horseback; and the sun being excessively hot, at noon and night we were, of course, much exhausted. At such times two or three grains of quinine soon wrought a happy change in our feelings. Quinine taken as a precaution, or an (almost) preventer of fever, is an invaluable medicine everywhere in the tropics. It is a powerful tonic, and if used in moderation it strengthens and builds up the system, leaving no unpleasant effects, no depressing reaction; besides, a large quantity may be carried in small bulk, and with the addition of a little water, or even taken dry, it is always in readiness for immediate use.

On the 1st of February we passed the boundaries of ancient Cambodia. The Siamese have at different times appropriated so much of this territory that from being one of the largest of the Indo-Chinese countries it has become the smallest. The Annamites also, and latterly the French, have encroached upon its eastern and southern borders, and 'between two fires'—avoiding Scylla, falling upon Charybdis—the old kingdom of Khamen, or Kamboja, has suffered both much and long.

Our daily routine of marching and camping is quite simple. We rarely accomplish more than twenty miles a day, and at night sleep under a large tree, with naught but the blue, star-studded canopy of heaven above us. At a night bivouac each of our attendants has his especial duty. The baggage and provision carts are usually two or three hours behind us, as we make about an hour more than they do on the road. If we are so fortunate as to obtain an old *sala* for the night, the carts are driven to its side, and the drivers at once unyoke the oxen and lead them off to graze at the edge of the forest. Our butler and one of the 'boys' then removes from the carts our respective mattresses, which are placed upon the *sala* floor side by side; our books, writing materials, and personal baggage most in request soon follow. 'Deng,' the Chinese cook, assisted by 'Tuh,' one of the Siamese 'boys,' builds the fire and begins to prepare the dinners. The fireplaces are rather ingeniously made. Two holes are dug near each other in the hard clay and united underneath the surface; the one is round, larger below than above, in fact—its mouth will just receive a kettle or saucepan—the other is bored in an oblong direction, sloping up to the surface. This is the 'draught,' and through this aperture the fire is fed with light, dry fuel. 'Imm,' the Chinese butler, soon has our table 'set,' i.e. the plates and dishes are placed on a large bamboo mat upon the floor, and before long the meal itself is thus announced: 'Master, master, dinny have got leady.' But prior to this our dusty travelling clothes have been removed, we have bathed, and dressed in clean and cool *baju* and *pyjamas* (loose jacket and drawers of thin silk or linen), and we now recline at length upon our beds, much after the manner of the ancient Romans at their *symposia*,—and partake of the frugal repast. Our larder is modest but sufficient, for besides tinned provisions and a variety of liquors we obtain such fresh food as eggs, rice, fish, poultry, and fruit by official levies upon the country people.

On our *menu* there will often be, as a starter (or 'preliminary canter,' as an Englishman rendered the Parisian *hors d'œuvre* of breakfast), oyster soup, the oysters *bonâ fide*; next roast beef, green peas, and potatoes for the substantials; egg curry and rice with preserved tamarinds will do duty as *entremets*; stewed pippins, dried figs, and bread and butter serve for dessert; and as beverages—on the wine list—we have sherry-wine, beer, claret, and brandy; and then, as a fit conclusion of the whole matter, *café noir*. After dinner there is a general talk of the day's travel, or else some one reads a few pages of Mark Twain, or Artemus Ward, or Dr. Holmes, and then, after a look at the animals, we go 'to roost'—*literally*, for the partial flooring of the *sala* is four or five feet above the ground—usually by nine o'clock, for we need rest, and prefer to begin our march by daylight, and thus employ the coolest part of the day. The 'boys' build large fires on every side of the *sala* to frighten away wild animals, to keep themselves warm (for the nights are cold in comparison with the days), also to provide light and guard against thieves, and to drive off mosquitoes by the smoke.

Watchmen are appointed, each 'boy' in turn, to protect the oxen and ponies. Our attendants sleep upon the bare ground, with their entire persons enveloped with blankets or coarse sheets, to shield themselves from mosquitoes or any poisonous insects. If there is no *sala* at hand, a circle is made of our carts (about which the men sleep) around a large tree, under which we sleep, and then with an outer cordon of fire we consider ourselves pretty safe. In the mornings, while the General is marshalling the caravan, and the missionary is recording, in a blank-book, his impressions of life and adventure in the interior of Siam, there is usually opportunity to use the pencil; and, seated upon the ground, with a drawing-book in hand, I make rough sketches of the country, people, and their characteristics — now an image of Budha, then a *wat*, a Cambodian nobleman, or a particularly romantic camp, a cart, an elephant, or perhaps a *sala* — where no photographer or artist has been before me.

Passing slowly through an immense plain of grass six feet in height, with large burned tracts here and there, we approached the town of Sesupon. Around the bases of some large trees, usually a group of three or four, we saw hillocks ten feet in height and eighty feet in circumference, the habitations of a species of white ant.

These are built so large and high in order to avoid the effects—floods—of the annual rain, as in some parts of tropical America a species of black ant builds large nests—roundish, of light earth and plastered smooth— on trees for the same purpose. The Governor of Sesupon was very demonstrative in his wishes to be of all possible service to us. He provided for our use three elephants and three buffalo and one bullock cart. He sent us presents also of fresh pork, onions, rice, eggs, sugar, and some very nice vermicelli made from rice flour. During our first interview His Excellency smoked three cigars and drank a dozen little cups of tea, but declined some brandy which we proffered, saying he was not accustomed to its use. Europeans very seldom visit this part of Siam, and we were, therefore, objects of great curiosity to the natives, who crowded in upon all sides of our *sala* to view the ' farangs.' In the Governor's garden were some green stuffs, such as onions, cabbages, salads, &c., and all about we could see evidences of the great fertility of the soil, and that the natives were too lazy to cultivate anything more than the bare necessities of life, and selected even of them those which required the least possible exertion for a return. There were in Sesupon some excellent fat pigs, and also some very sleek-looking cattle. European or American settlers might do well in many parts of the country, were it not for the hot climate and the malignant fevers which are so prevalent during a great part of the year.

The elephants we obtained at this town were rather smaller than the average of those seen in India. The Siamese howdah, or elephant saddle, also differs from that used by the Hindoos. It is simply an oblong wooden box (five feet in length, two and a half in width, and one foot in depth), which fits snugly to the elephant's back; it has a circular bamboo top or cover, five or six feet in height, which rises from the two ends, and has curtains provided for both the front and rear sides. Under it upon the monster's back are placed, first, a thick sheet of soft bark, and then three or four pieces of stiff raw hide, and the saddle is secured by a rattan rope, about an inch in diameter, passed under the belly, by a rope crupper to the tail, and forwards by ropes round the animal's massive neck. The mahout, or driver, sits of course upon the neck, his feet and legs placed against the ears, by which in great part he guides the beast; though the Siamese elephant is accustomed to no words of command—' to the right ' or left, ' advance,' ' stop,' &c.—nor to kneel when about to be mounted, as in India. In riding one may either sit cross-legged upon soft cushions or rest as in a chair, placing the feet upon the animal's neck. In some parts of Siam a young elephant may be purchased for as little as twenty *ticals* (about $12). The animals which we had

SIAMESE WAR ELEPHANT

from time to time travelled two, or two and a half miles an hour, but they could not make more than twenty miles a day, nor could they carry more than four hundred pounds' weight upon their backs.

One day, near a lake where we had been resting

during the great heat of noon, the missionary discovered some interesting ruins—large blocks of a grey stone, with *basso-relievo* carving upon them. We had met with many Cambodians during the past week: their appearance is very like that of the Siamese; their houses are similar in construction; they worship the same Budha; their manners and customs are identical; their laws have the same tenor; but their languages are very dissimilar. We had an opportunity of seeing some natives fishing in a small river near the town of Panoum-sok. While we were resting in the *sala* after tiffin, some two hundred men, women, and children came out from their huts and entered the river—here about one hundred and fifty feet in width and from two to six feet in depth—together, and while some drew nets, the majority used a sort of trap, made of bamboo, three feet in length, open at one end the entire diameter (about a foot) and closed at the other, excepting a hole in the centre of sufficient size to receive the arm. This trap was quickly thrust down to the bed of the river, and the number and size of the fish ensnared by such simple means was a source of much astonishment to us all; many of them would weigh three pounds.

At Panoum-sok we were housed in a most excellent

SIAMESE GENTLEMAN AND LADY

sala, and everything was done for our comfort by an under-governor. While we were at dinner there came an imposing procession of fourteen men, women, and children, walking in single file, headed by two of the chief men of the town, and bringing in their hands and on their heads presents of food in almost endless variety; there was rice, two kinds of dried fish, pork, eggs (fresh), *salted* eggs (prepared in native style), bananas (Siamese), cooked dinners, and one little table which had upon it five different kinds of cakes and sweets; some of these latter we ate after dinner, and found them quite palatable. These good (except the *salted eggs*—ugh!) things were sent us by the Governor's wife, His Excellency being absent on a journey to Korat for the purpose of assisting at the cremation ceremonies of his dead nephew.

The Governor's wife intended herself to leave in the morning for Siamrap to attend the marriage of her cousin there, and she very courteously invited us to join her party. But upon learning that it was her intention to travel slowly, we were obliged to decline her invitation, for we had already been too much delayed upon the road. After dinner came four more presents of food, making twenty-two in all: we appropriated some delicacies for our own use, but gave the greater part to our attendants, who, it is almost needless to add, lived extremely well, or 'high,' according to their own dietetic philosophy, during the entire journey from Bangkok.

CHAPTER XVI.

SIAMRAP

At about eleven o'clock on the morning of the 11th we came suddenly upon a branch of the Kmpong-Seng river, which is here spanned by an old, ruined stone bridge, about three hundred feet in length, sixty in height, and forty in width. It is built of a very coarse porous stone—evidently of volcanic origin—with twenty-six arches in the pointed Gothic style of architecture; it rests upon a massive platform of masonry, and the blocks of stone—four feet in length, two in breadth, and one in thickness—are laid entirely without cement. There is no carving to be seen except a little arabesque work upon the narrow stone coping. No keystone being employed, and the stones not being smoothed upon their tops, the arches have consequently many of them broken in, and all are much dilapidated. The bridge exhibits marks of great age; most of the stone facing has been thrown down; the top of the bridge is overgrown with shrubs, and in one or two places quite large trees have grown up, fastening their roots into the rich *débris* between the blocks of stone. Some of these latter have been worn round and nearly smooth, by the action of running water apparently; many blocks have small holes in them, as if by this means they had been lifted and placed in position. There are no other ruins to be seen near the bridge except two small heaps of stone and rubbish in the centre of a shallow lake. This bridge, which the natives in their flowery diction style *Taphan-theph*—the 'Celestial,' 'Angels',' or 'Shining Bridge' (as it may be variously translated)—was probably built about the same time as the temples and palaces of Angkor, when that city was the capital of Cambodia —many hundred years since.

We crossed *Taphan-theph* upon our elephants, and soon after halted for tiffin under the shade of some large trees. In the afternoon I had a long ride in one of the little passenger bullock-carts. The body of this vehicle looks very much like a huge barrel; it is made of bamboo covered with leaves, but so narrow is it that one has to sit cross-legged, and so low is it that when thus sitting it is impossible to wear one's hat. Upon a small seat which projects out before, the driver sits; he drives the oxen by means of a small rope passed through their nostrils, and uses a goad (a sharp nail fastened to the extremity of a stout stick) upon their humps instead of a lash. The bullocks usually bear strings of wooden clapper-bells around their necks, and when trotting fast their jingling sound reminds one somewhat of the sleigh-bells in winter at home. Upon a good, level road this mode of conveyance is not disagreeable, but little of the country through which one is riding can, however, be seen.

Siamrap we found to be a town—of about a thousand inhabitants—pleasantly situated upon the banks of a small river, and three and a half miles distant from the ruins at Angkor. We were received in the public *sala* by the *Palat* (an inferior provincial officer), who brought us an invitation from the Governor to dine with him; but this hospitality we were obliged to decline, feeling quite exhausted after our day's travel. It seemed that we had arrived in Siamrap at a time of unusual festivity. The daughter of the Governor was about to be married to the cousin of the Governor of Battambong—a large province to the south-west—and great preparations for the happy event were going forwards. After we had unpacked some of the baggage the Governor sent us a very nice

Siamese (though served in European style) dinner upon a silver tray; there was soup in a large blue China tureen, a great dish of boiled rice, and a variety of stewed meats and condiments in small bowls: knives and forks were provided and a table and chairs brought, a cloth laid, and upon it (*mirabile visu!*) a 'reg'lar down-east' tallow-dip was placed, the the wick being quite two-thirds of its size, and it burning at *about* the rate of an inch a minute. After dinner we had a long conversation, through 'Henry' as medium, with the chief men of the village, who asked questions—many very absurd ones too—much faster than we could answer them. In the morning came presents from the Governor of a shoulder of beef, some eggs, fowls, cucumbers, pumelows, and bananas. We sent our letter from the Foreign Office at Bangkok to His Excellency. It was received with distinguished ceremony on a golden salver, with a conspicuous display of white umbrellas; and afterwards we were invited to an interview.

In the river near the *sala* are several large water-wheels, used by the natives for drawing water by the action of the current of the stream. Their construction is novel; the wheels are perhaps twelve feet in diameter, with broad flanges made of mats, the action of the current turning them, and the water of the river, directed to this point, filling small joints of bamboo which are fastened to the inner circumference of the wheel, and these, revolving, are emptied upon a thatch of *atap*-palm leaves, a trough under which collects the water, which is then directed to the different houses by means of long wooden pipes. Lower down the river were several canoes and barges, hollowed out of single trunks of trees, which were as much as forty feet in length and eight feet in beam or breadth; one had a cabin of palm leaves built in its centre, and a grass thatch extending over it from stem to stern. These canoes and large boats are intended rather for use on Lake Thalaysap, eight miles distant, being too unwieldy and of too great draught to penetrate far up the river.

The walls of Siamrap, built of brick and stone, are twelve feet in height and about half a mile in circumference; they have bastions at the corners, and openings in the parapet for cannon. The Governor afterwards told the General that forty years ago each of these embrasures—there are 806 of them—was occupied by a cannon, but having since become rusty and otherwise out of repair, they have all been removed. There are two gates on the eastern side and one on each of the others. These gateways are surrounded by curious old towers or guard-rooms, with peaked roofs; the gates themselves are built of massive teak planks, thickly studded with large iron nails. There are few houses besides the palace and the courts of justice within the walls; the town, which is not very large, lies chiefly along the banks of the small river which flows south to the Lake Thalaysap, on the eastern side of the walls. The houses, built upon piles, of bamboo and palm-leaf, and thatched with grass, and the people seem generally to present a more thrifty appearance than that usual in Siamese villages.

Preceded by the interpreter and followed by all our servants, we entered the palace enclosure through one of the immense gates already mentioned, and walked fearlessly past the gaping mouth of a large iron cannon, mounted upon huge wooden wheels; for we knew no danger was to be apprehended, since the bore of the cannon had been converted into a peaceful aviary. The Governor received us in a long and broad verandah and waved us graciously to some chairs, himself taking one before us. Behind His Excellency, laid upon the floor, were some red velvet cushions, elegantly embroidered with gold thread, and before them were placed the most magnificent betel-boxes, cigar-cases, spittoons, &c., we had as yet seen; they were made of pure Siamese gold and studded with costly gems. There was also a set of beautiful tea-things. Along the walls of the verandah or audience hall were placed rows of guns and swords; some of the former were old-fashioned flint-locks, some were modern muskets of good manufacture, some were furnished with bayonets—rather formidable-looking weapons—and with brass scabbards. At the right of His Excellency were some royal umbrellas in cases, some long state swords to be carried in procession, a Connecticut clock, some glass candlesticks and shades, &c., and the walls were hung with grotesque Chinese paintings. Grouped about the Governor, to the right and left, were some hundred or more prostrate officers and attendants; the rank of each might be determined by his dress, the material of which his betel-boxes were manufactured, and the proximity to his lord. The Governor was a young man—a Cambodian by birth—of pleasant though not very intellectual countenance, of short stature, inclined to obesity; and he was dressed in a white under-vest, stand-up collar with a gold button, a yellow figured silk gown, and a green silk *panoung*, the lower part of the legs and his feet being bare. His Excellency promised to provide elephants to carry the General and the missionary back to Sesupon and Kabin when they were ready to return, and also to give me a letter of introduction to the Prime Minister of Cambodia, requesting him to obtain for me, if possible, an audience with His Majesty the King of Cambodia, and also to provide a boat and boatmen to convey me across Lake Thalaysap and down the Mesap river to Panompin, the capital.

During the interview the Governor ordered his own band of fourteen instruments to play for our amusement. Cambodian music, like the Siamese, consists principally of *noise*—of the shrill and penetrating sounds produced by flageolets and other peculiarly formed reed instruments, and the banging, clanging, and rattling of tom-toms, cymbals, musical wheels (metal cups of different sizes and thicknesses struck with a hammer), bamboo sticks (also of different sizes and thicknesses, and struck in the same manner); all playing their loudest, most interminable notes in full blast at the same time, and for half an hour without intermission. The character of the music, however, is often sweet, sometimes wailing and rather dirge-like, although always played in quick time. The instruments themselves are capable of considerable melody, if played with reference to tune and time, modulation and expression. The performers upon the musical wheels and the boxes with suspended bamboo sticks evinced much skill in the use of their instruments. When playing the musicians sit upon the floor in rows

CAMBODIAN FEMALE BAND

close together; there does not appear to be any particular leader, as there is no particular tune. On taking leave, the Governor sent with us a present of water-melons, pumelows, jack-fruits, and bananas.

The total distance we travelled from Bangkok was 275 miles; of this 30 miles was by canal in boats, 30 miles on the Bang pa Kong river in boats, and the remainder—215 miles—was performed upon horses and elephants, in bullock-carts, and on foot; the greater part of the journey, however, was accomplished on horseback. The time consumed in making this trip was seventeen days.

The Governor of Siamrap having provided us with three elephants, on the 13th inst. we started for the ruins of Angkor, three and a half miles distant, to the north. We took but little baggage with us, being rather impatient now that we were nearing the main object of the expedition—the *ultima Thule* of our desires and hopes—and so we passed quickly and silently along a narrow but good road cut through the dense, *riant* forest, until, in about an hour's time, on suddenly emerging from the woods, we saw a little way off to the right, across a pond filled with lotus plants, a long row of columned galleries, and beyond—high above the beautiful cocoa and areca palms—three or four immense pagodas, built of a dark-grey stone. And my heart almost bounded into my mouth as the Cambodian driver, turning towards the howdah, said, with a bright flush of the eye and a proud turn of the lip, '*Naghon Wat;*' for we were then at the very portals of the famous old 'City of Monasteries,' and not far distant was *Angkorthôm*—Angkor the Great.

ANGKOR WAT: ENTRANCE WEST OF THE FIRST ENCEINTE: INNER VIEW

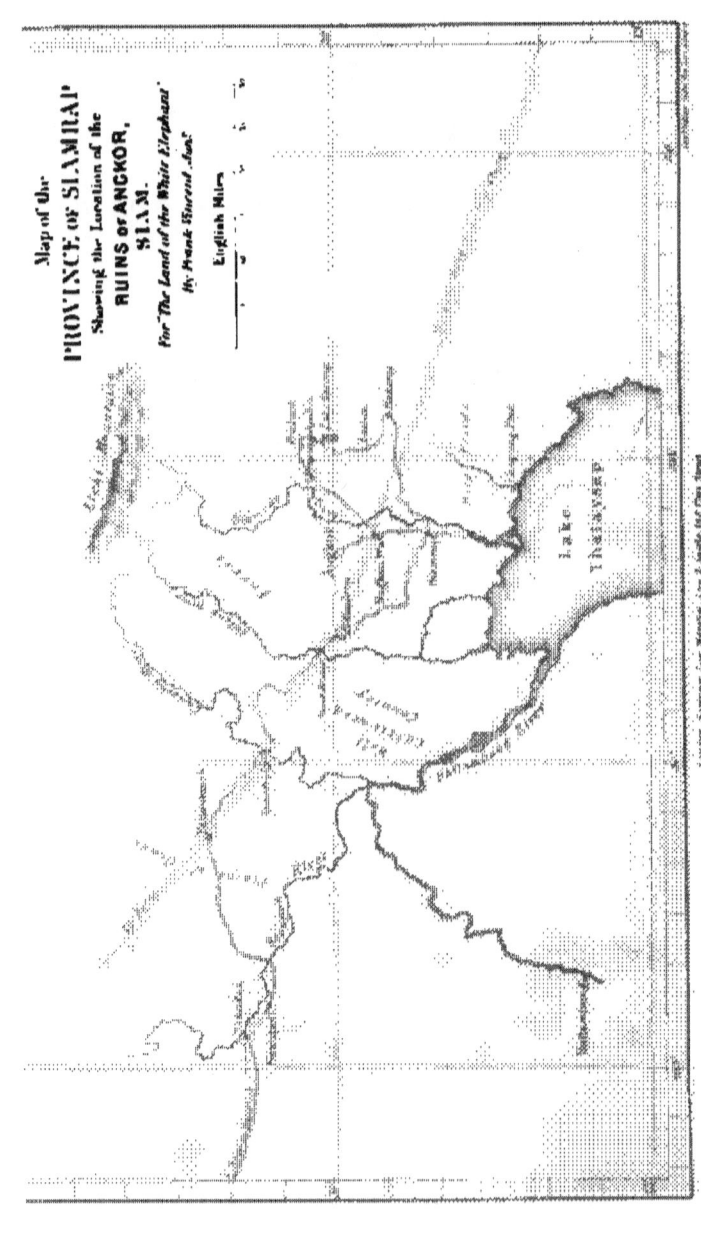

CHAPTER XVII.

THE RUINS OF ANGKOR—THE GREAT TEMPLE

WE, whose good fortune it is to live in the nineteenth century, are accustomed to boast of the perfection and pre-eminence of our modern civilisation, of the grandeur of our attainments in Science, Art, Literature, and what not, as compared with those whom we call ancients; but still we are compelled to admit that they have far excelled our recent endeavours in many things, and notably in the Fine Arts of painting, architecture, and sculpture. We were but just looking upon a most wonderful example of the two latter, for in style and beauty of architecture, solidity of construction, and magnificent and elaborate carving and sculpture, the great *Nagkon Wat* has no superior, certainly no rival, standing at the present day. The first view of the ruins is almost overwhelming. One writer says, 'The ruins of Angkor are as imposing as the ruins of Thebes or Memphis, and more mysterious;' and another—M. Monhot—whose work we have used as a guide-book in this distant part of Siam—thinks that ' one of these temples [*Nagkon Wat*]—a rival to that of Solomon, and erected by some ancient Michael Angelo—might take an honourable place beside our most beautiful buildings. It is grander than anything left to us by Greece or Rome.' At a first sight one is most impressed with the magnitude, minute detail, high finish, and elegant proportions of this temple, and then to the bewildered beholder arise mysterious after-thoughts—who built it? when was it built? and where now are its builders? But it is doubtful if these questions will ever be answered. There exist no credible traditions—all is absurd fable or legend.

The ruins of Angkor are situated in the province of Siamrap, eastern Siam, in about Lat. 13.30 N. and Long. 104 E. We entered upon an immense causeway, the stairs of which were flanked with six huge griffins, each carved from a single block of stone. This causeway, which leads directly to the main entrance of the temple, is 725 feet in length, and is paved with stones which each measures four feet in length by two in breadth. On either side of it are artificial lakes fed by springs, and each covering about five acres of ground. We passed through one of the side gates and crossed the square to a *sala* situated at the very

entrance of the temple. Embosomed in the midst of a perfect forest of cocoa, betel-nut, and toddy palms, and with no village in sight—excepting a dozen or more huts, the abodes of priests having the charge of

PRIEST'S HOUSE, NAOKON WAT.

it—the general appearance of the wonderful temple is beautiful and romantic as well as impressive and grand. A just idea of it can hardly be conveyed by writing; it must be seen to be understood and appreciated. Still, perhaps, a detailed description might assist the imagination somewhat in forming a proper estimate of the grand genius which planned and the skill and patience which executed such a masterpiece of architecture.

The outer wall of *Nagkon Wat*—which words signify a city or assemblage of temples or monasteries—about half a mile square, is built of sandstone, with gateways upon each side, which are handsomely carved with figures of gods and dragons, arabesques and intricate scrolls. Upon the western side is the main gateway, and passing through this and up a causeway (paved with slabs of stone three feet in length by two in breadth) for a distance of a thousand feet, you arrive at the central main entrance of the temple. About the middle of the causeway, on either side, are image-houses, much decayed and overgrown with rank parasitic plants; and a little farther on are two small ponds, with carved stone copings, which in most places are thrown down. The foundations of *Nagkon Wat* are as much as ten feet in height, and are very massively built of the same volcanic rock as that used in the construction of the 'Angels' Bridge.' The entire edifice—which is raised on three terraces, the one about thirty feet above the other—including the roof, is of stone, but without cement, and so closely-fitting are the joints

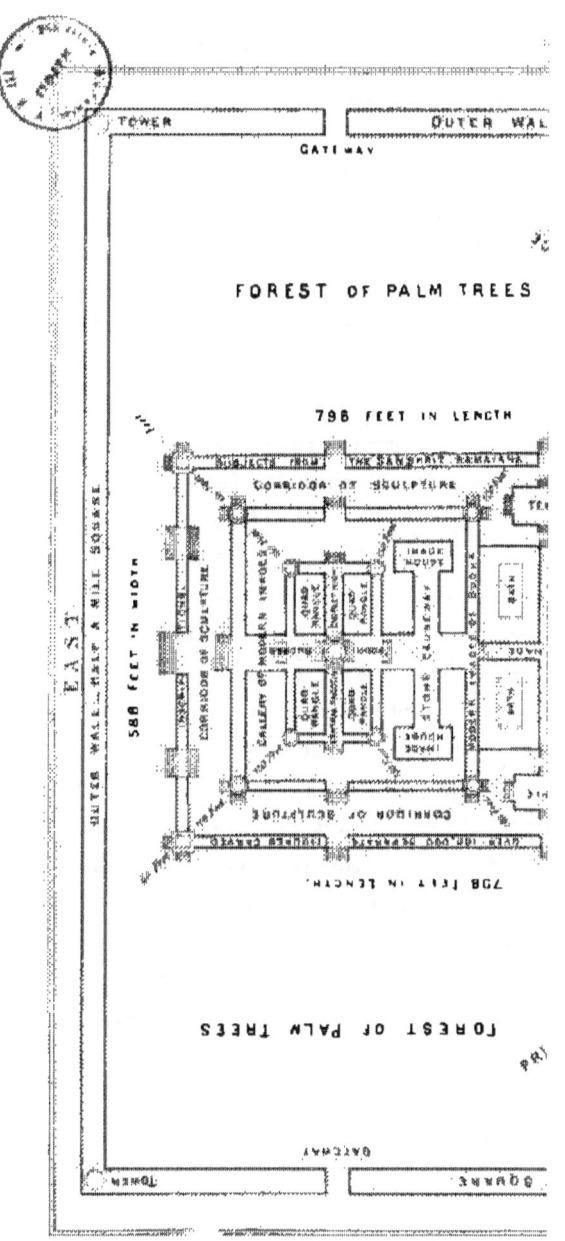

as even now to be scarcely discernible. The quarry where the stone was hewn is about two days' travel—thirty miles—distant, and it is supposed the transportation of the immense boulders could only have been effected by means of a water communication—a canal or river, or when the country was submerged at the end of the rainy season. The shape of the building is oblong, being 796 feet in length and 588 feet in width, while the highest central pagoda rises some 250 odd feet above the ground, and four others, at the angles of the court, are each about 150 feet in height.

Passing between low railings, we ascend a platform—composed of boulders of stone four feet in length, one and a half feet in width, and six inches in thickness—and enter the temple itself through a columned portico, the *façade* of which is beautifully carved in *basso-relievo* with ancient mythological subjects. From this doorway, on either side, runs a corridor with a double row of columns, cut—base and capital—from single blocks, with a double, oval-shaped roof covered with carving and consecutive sculptures upon the outer wall. This gallery of sculptures, which forms the exterior of the temple, consists of over half a mile of continuous pictures, cut in *basso-relievo* upon sandstone slabs six feet in width, and represents subjects

taken from Hindoo mythology—from the *Ramayana*—
the Sanscrit epic poem of India—with its 25,000 verses
describing the exploits of the god Rama and the son
of the King of Oudh. The contests of the King of
Ceylon, and Hanuman, the monkey god, are gra-

SCULPTURES IN THE CITY OF ANGKOR.

phically represented. There is no keystone used in
the arch of this corridor, and its ceiling is uncarved.
On the walls are sculptured the immense number of
100,000 separate figures (or at least heads). Entire
scenes from the *Ramayana* are pictured; one, I re-
member, occupies 240 feet of the wall. Weeks might

be spent in studying, identifying, and classifying the varied subjects of this wonderful gallery. You see warriors riding upon elephants and in chariots, foot soldiers with shield and spear, boats, unshapely divinities, trees, monkeys, tigers, griffins, hippopotami, serpents, fishes, crocodiles, bullocks, tortoises, soldiers of immense physical development, with helmets, and some people with beards—probably Moors. The figures stand somewhat like those on the great Egyptian monuments, the side partly turned towards the front; in the case of the men one foot and leg are always placed in advance of the other; and I noticed, besides, five horsemen, armed with spear and sword, riding abreast, like those seen upon the Assyrian tablets in the British Museum.

. In the processions several of the kings are preceded by musicians playing upon shells and long bamboo flutes. Some of the kings carry a sort of battle-axe, others a weapon which much resembles a golf-club, and others are represented as using the bow and arrow. In one place is a grotesque divinity who sits elegantly dressed upon a throne surmounted by umbrellas; this figure, of peculiar sanctity evidently, has been recently gilded, and before it, upon a small table, there were a dozen or more 'joss-sticks' kept constantly burning by the faithful. But it is almost useless to particularise when the subjects and style of execution are so diverse. Each side of the long corridor seemed to display figures of distinct feature, dress, and character 'The most interesting sculptures,' says Dr. Adolf Bastian, the President of the Royal Geographical Society of Berlin, who explored these wonderful ruins in 1864, 'the most interesting sculptures at *Nagkon Wat* are in two compartments, called by the natives respectively the procession and the three stages (heaven, earth, and hell). What gives a peculiar interest to this section is the fact that the artist has represented the different nationalities in all their distinctive characteristic features, from the flat-nosed savage in the tasseled garb of the Pnom and the short haired Lao to the straight-nosed Rajaput, with sword and shield, and the bearded Moor, giving a catalogue of nationalities, like another column of Trajan, in the predominant physical conformation of each race. On the whole there is such a prevalence of Hellenic cast in the features and profiles, as well as in the elegant attitude of the horsemen, that one might suppose Xenocrates of old, after finishing his labours in Bombay, had made an excursion to the east.'

There are figures sculptured in high relief (nearly life-size) upon the lower parts of the walls about the

SCULPTURES AT NAGKON WAT

SCULPTURES AT ENTRANCE TO NAOKON WAT

entrance; all are females, and apparently of Hindoo origin. The interior of the quadrangle bounded by

NAGKON WAT COLUMNS

the long corridor just described is filled with galleries—halls, formed with huge columns, crossing one another at right angles. In the *Naykon Wat* as many as 1,532 solid columns have been counted, and among the entire ruins of Angkor there are reported to be the immense number of 6,000, almost all of them hewn from single blocks and artistically carved. On the inner side of the corridor there are blank windows, each of which contains seven beautifully turned little columns. The ceilings of the galleries were hung with tens of thousands of bats and pigeons, and other birds had made themselves comfortable nests in out-of-the-way corners. We pass on up steep staircases, with steps not more than four inches in width, to the centre of the galleries which here bisect one another. There are two detached buildings in this square, probably used formerly as image-houses, and they now contain wooden Budhas, though of recent date. In one of the galleries we saw two or three hundred images—made of stone, wood, brass, clay—of all shapes and sizes and ages (some of the large stone idols are said to be 1,400 years old), a Budha's 'sacred foot,' &c.; 'joss-sticks' were burning before the largest images, which were besides daubed with red paint and partially gilded. We walk on across another causeway, with small image-houses on either hand, and up a steep flight of steps, fully thirty feet in height, to other galleries crossing each other in the

ANGKOR WAT: FRAGMENT OF BAS-RELIEF

centre, above which rises the grand central pagoda—250 feet in height—and at the four corners of the court four smaller spires. These latter are much dilapidated and do not now display their full height; the porticoes also bear evidence of the presence of the 'heavy hand of time.' Upon the four sides of the base of the highest spire are colossal images of Budha—made of plaster—and other smaller divinities in various positions. These figures of Budha are grandly placed, for when the doors of the enclosing rooms are opened, from their high position they overlook the surrounding country; and the priests of *Naykon Wat* worship here at the present day. There is one more gallery, and then we come to the outer corridor, and pass through a magnificent doorway to the rear of the temple, and walk round to our *sala*, not knowing which to admire the most, the vastness of the plan or the propriety and grace of the performance.

But who built the *Naykon Wat?* and when was it built? Learned men (who have visited the ruins) have attempted to form opinions from studies of its construction and especially its ornamentation; but what decision could be reached, what judgment passed, when we see in the same temple carved images of Budha, four- and even thirty-two-armed, and two- and sixteen-headed gods, the Indian Vishnu, gods *with wings*, Burmese heads, Hindoo figures, Ceylon mythology, &c.? Native Cambodian historians reckon 2,400 years from the building of *Nagkon Wat*, and the traditions of their country are said to date back to the year of the world 205. Some have supposed *Nagkon Wat* to be but 1,400 years old, to have been built by different kings, and to have been completed by one who was a Budhist. The Cambodians still possess accounts of the introduction of Budhism. 'Samanokodom left Ceylon and went to Tibet, where he was very well received; from thence he went among the savages, but not meeting with encouragement from them, he took refuge in Cambodia, where he was welcomed by the people.' And Dr. Bastian says that this temple was built for the reception of the learned patriarch Buddhaghosa, who brought the holy books of the *Trai-Pidok* from Langka (Ceylon). And likewise Bishop Pallegoix, a French Roman Catholic missionary who resided many years in Siam, travelled much about the country, and wrote a very valuable work upon Siam and the Siamese, refers the erection of this edifice to the reign of Phra Pathum Suriving, at the time the sacred books of the Budhists were brought from Ceylon and Budhism became the religion of the Cambodians. The natives

COLONNADE AT NAGKON WAT

THE GRAND STAIRCASE, NAGKON WAT

themselves (the common people) can throw no light upon this subject. I asked one of them how long *Naykon Wat* had been built. 'None can tell when—many hundred years ago,' he replied. I asked if Cambodians or some other race erected this wonderful building, and he answered frankly, 'I do not know; but it must have either sprung up from the ground or been built by giants, or perhaps by the angels.' Another man said he did not believe it was built by angels, for he could see the effect of the tools of man upon it—certainly an amazing display of intellectual acumen for a native. But still the degenerate Cambodians of the present day, whose only genius expresses itself in the carving of their boats, have no idea or belief that their ancestors may have constructed these temples.

'Was civilisation,' asks Louis de Carné (late member of the French Commission of Exploration of the Makong river)—'was civilisation, in the complex meaning we give that word, in keeping among the ancient Cambodians with what such prodigies of architecture seem to indicate? The age of Phidias was that of Sophocles, Socrates, and Plato; Michael Angelo and Raphael succeeded Dante. There are luminous epochs during which the human mind, developing itself in every direction, triumphs in all, and creates masterpieces which spring from the same inspiration. Have the nations of India ever known such periods of special glory? It appears little probable, and it is only necessary to read the Chinese traveller of the thirteenth century, whose narrative M. Abel Rémusat has translated, to be convinced that it was never reached by the Khmers [ancient Cambodians]. He describes the monuments of the capital, most of which were covered with gilding, and he adds that, with the exception of the temples and the palace, all the houses were only thatched. Their size was regulated by the rank of the possessor, but the richest did not venture to build one like that of any of the great officers of state. Despotism induced corruption of manners, and some customs mentioned by our author show actual barbarism.' This article would tend to prove, therefore, that the authorship of *Naykon Wat* must be ascribed to other than the ancient Cambodians. But to whom?

M. Henri Mouhot, who gave the first exact account of these since celebrated ruins, was strongly of the opinion that they were built by some of the lost tribes of Israel—those scape-goats of so many anonymous monuments throughout the world. M. Mouhot, in his travels through Indo-China, made many efforts to discover traces of Jewish emigration to Siam or Cambodia, but met with nothing satisfactory excepting a record of the Judgment of Solomon—attributed to one of their kings, who had become a god after having been, according to their ideas of metempsychosis, an ape, an elephant, &c.—which was found by M. Miche, the French Bishop of Laos and Cambodia, to be preserved *verbatim* in one of the Cambodian sacred books. Everywhere M. Mouhot was told 'there were no Jews in the country;' still he could not but be struck by the Hebrew character of the faces of many of the savage Stiens, and when looking at the figures in the bas-reliefs at Angkor, he could not avoid remarking the strong resemblance of the faces there to those of these savages. 'And besides the similar regularity of feature, there are the same long beards, straight *langoutis* (waistcloths), and even the same weapons and musical instruments.' It is M. Mouhot's belief that, without exaggeration, some of the oldest parts of Angkor may be fixed at more than 2,000 years ago, and the more recent portions not much later. But where are now the race of people who had the genius to plan and the skill and patience to rear such magnificent structures? There is no trace of them existing among the Cambodians of the present day; there is no trace of any such people among the surrounding nations, unless, indeed, faith is to be placed in the statement concerning the Stiēns, and another race—the Bannaus—quite as well, who inhabit the old country Chiampa, or Tciampa. And the Abbé Jaquenet, a Roman Catholic missionary in Cochin China, seems rather to confirm M. Mouhot's impressions, for he writes: 'Whether we consider the commercial relations of the Jews with these countries, particularly when, in the height of their power, the combined fleets of Solomon and Hiram went to seek the treasures of Ophir (a generic name used, perhaps, to designate the two Indies), or whether we come lower down, to the dispersion of the ten tribes, who, instead of returning from captivity, set out from the banks of the Euphrates and reached the shores of the ocean—whatever ground of explanation we resolve upon,' concludes the pious father, 'the shining of the light of revelation in the far east is not the less incontestable.' Another circumstance of considerable interest, and one mentioned by both Dr. Bastian and M. Mouhot, is, that the foundation of Angkor is referred by the native historians to a Prince of Roma, or Ruma, and that the name of Roma is familiar to nearly all the Cambodians, who place it at the western end of the world.

VIEW FROM CENTRAL PAGODA: KAOKOK WAY

We regarded the temples as at least a thousand years old; for how could a race be swept entirely—with not a single vestige—out of existence in less time? And again, the general appearance of the buildings—the deeply-worn stone stairs, the battered and decayed columns and slabs, the moss-covered and fallen roof, the absence of the keystone in the arches, and the undecipherable inscriptions, all betoken great age, giving evidence of another people and another civilisation. The style of the architecture of this *wat* is very like that of the temples of India, and somewhat resembles also that of the temples of Java, and this would, perhaps, seem to indicate a Hindoo or a Malay origin; there is little resemblance, however, to the Egyptian monuments: here all is light, airy, graceful; there all is massive, severe, and grand.

But are there no tablets eulogising its founders or commemorating its establishment, no inscriptions concerning the building and the builders, set up in this temple? Yes, inscriptions truly there are; some can be deciphered and some can not, but those which can be read only give descriptions of offerings made by different donors, with some allusions to religious ceremonies and mythological objects. There is a tablet of black marble, about five feet square, let into the wall of the rear (eastern) corridor, from which this information, and this alone, may be gained. The inscriptions which cannot be read are written in ancient Cambodian, in a character which resembles the Pali, though in a more antiquated form. 'The language differs from the vernacular Cambodian, as well as from the Pali, and is not understood now.' It is said that several of the old kings of Cambodia 'introduced compulsory changes into the alphabet,' besides changing the Cambodian era, and hence we see the almost hopeless confusion which Orientalists now have to encounter and overcome before the chronology and history of this country can be known. And there we must leave this interesting question until some inscriptions are discovered which, with competent linguists to decipher them, may offer something of historical moment, or until some monastery may be found which has preserved a record of these very 'problematic annals'—*if indeed they have ever been written.*

An officer of the Chinese Government visited the capital of Cambodia in the year 1295, and mentions the wonderful appearance of the city and its monuments, and describes some of the manners and customs of the people. From this traveller's time until the latter part of the sixteenth century nothing authentic

ANGLE OF THE GREAT COURT OF THE TEMPLE

is heard. Christoval de Jaque, a Portuguese, who in 1570, being driven from Japan, took refuge in Cambodia, describes the ruins of *Nagkon Wat*, and states that even then the inscriptions were unintelligible to the Cambodians, and that Angkor was no longer a royal residence. 'He seems to say that even at that period it had already been deserted by its inhabitants.' Christoval thought the Cambodians were the most potent people between the provinces of Pegu (Burma) and Tonquin (Annam). Perhaps the name 'Roma,' so familiar to all Cambodians, was introduced by the Portuguese through the tenets of the Roman Catholic faith; but then why should their religion have become extinct, and still the tradition of a Prince of Roma remain? Then again there is a long silence concerning these ruins, which is not broken until the year 1855; since which date the labours and studies of M. Mouhot, Dr. Bastian, and Mr. Thompson (the English photographer) have again brought the wonderful temples to the attention of the civilised world, and almost, as it were, discovered them for the first time, for it was to their persevering efforts mainly we were indebted for a knowledge of the ruins of Angkor and the great temple *Nagkon Wat*.

CHAPTER XVIII.

A CAMBODIAN MARRIAGE FESTIVAL.

THE principal ruins of Siam and Cambodia yet discovered lie in the province of Siamrap, as already stated. At about three miles north-east of Angkor, on the opposite side of the Siamrap river, are the ruins of a city called Pentaphrohm, the citadel of Taphrohm, and near it is a *wat* styled *Phrakeoh*, or the Gem Tower, presenting the same combination of a royal and priestly residence as *Angkor* and *Nagkon Wat*. Some of these temples and palaces, with their columns, sculptures, and statues, are quite as interesting, though not so well preserved, as those at Angkor. About four miles east of *Nagkon Wat* are two other remains of antiquity—*Bakong* and *Lailan*. At the latter there are several images of Budha ' built up of bricks upon the freestone which forms the fundament and the lower stage. The bricks are exceedingly hard, and made in a manner not understood now by the people of the country. They are polished and laid upon each other in so neat a manner that no traces of mortar can be discovered.' In the province of Battambong, forty or fifty miles south-west from Siamrap town, there are also ruins—temples, monasteries, and palaces—and indeed the whole valley of the Makong river to the very borders of China is spread with ruins of more or less magnitude, beauty, and interest.

Near the monastery of *Phrakeoh* is an artificial lake called *Sasong* (the Royal Lake), built by the kings of Pentaphrohm, and surrounded with pleasure houses for their recreation. Dr. Bastian thinks that it must have been a work of immense labour, and that the whole population of Cambodia of to-day would scarcely be able to raise such a gigantic structure. The lake of *Sasong* he describes as being 'of oblong shape, about 2,000 feet broad and 4,000 feet long, and surrounded by a high embankment of solid masonry. Some of the blocks are fourteen to sixteen feet long and highly finished. In convenient places square platforms were built overhanging the water, with broad flights of steps leading down to it, and in such places the huge masses of stone laid on each other are embellished by delicate chisellings, bearing the figures of serpents, eagles, lions (in their fabulous shapes, as Naga, Kruth, Sinto) on the ends. In the middle of the lake is a small island with the remains of a former palace upon it. Of all the figures used for ornaments, that which recurs most frequently is that of the Naga; and the Chinese officer who visited Cambodia in 1295 describes already 'the pillars of the stone bridges adorned with serpents, each of which had nine heads.'

We had been but two or three days at the *Nagkon Wat*, when there came an invitation from the Governor to visit him at Siamrap. So mounting our elephants early in the morning, we returned to our old *sala*, not far distant from the palace gate. Soon after our arrival came the promised letter of introduction from the Governor of Siamrap to the Prime Minister of Cambodia, requesting him to obtain me an audience with His Majesty. It was written in the Cambodian language, though accompanied by a Siamese translation, which latter 'Henry,' the Consulate interpreter, rendered into literal English for my instruction and amusement. It read as follows:—

'The letter of Phraya-nu-pap-Tripoph, the Governor of the Province of Siamrap, sent to Phraya-Kralahome at the city of Panompin, stating that the American Consul brought a letter with the seal of Chow-Phraya-Pootarupai out to the Governor of the Province of Siamrap, the substance of which is as follows:—

A CAMBODIAN MARRIAGE FESTIVAL 231

Mr. the American Consul wished to travel to the ruins of *Naykon Wat* and *Naykon Thôm*, and if Mr. Consul wished to travel to any place whatever, let the Governor prepare everything that he requires (to see it). The American Consul also wishes to have Mr.———, an American citizen, go out [i.e. of this Province] to see the city of Panompin. I herewith send (transport) Mr.———, the American citizen, out [i.e. of this Province to Panompin] in accordance with the tenor of the letter of Chow-Phraya-Pootarupai. Will you please conduct Mr.——— up to have an audience with His Majesty Ong Somdetch Morodom Phrannrowdom?

'Given on Saturday, the ninth day of the waxing moon, the fourth month of the year of the goat, and the third year of the reign.'

(SEAL)

An invitation to dinner accompanied this letter, and we could not refuse the hospitality of the Governor so courteously proffered, though we took pains to eat a tolerably substantial meal before going, agreeably to the necessities—as regards quality and species, not quantity—of native dinners before experienced. His Excellency received us in a truly oriental style of (very) 'low neck and (very) short sleeves' dress, having nothing whatever upon his dusky person excepting a silk *panoung*, round the loins. Dinner was served on a small table in the audience hall; and with about a hundred noblemen and attendants, who lay around crouching on the floor, curious to see the *farangs*' barbarous and ridiculous manner of eating. The Governor had resided some time at Bangkok, and consequently had seen a good deal of foreigners and their customs, and so the dinner was served with all the western display his experience and *cuisine* could prompt or effect. The meal was presented in *five courses*—soups, meats, vegetables, sweets, and fruits— and the table was lavishly burdened with the variety of food. There were two kinds of soup, served in large blue china tureens; pigs' feet and boiled beef; broiled chicken, cooked spread out flat, *with the feet attached*; fried sweet potatoes (here a white variety); boiled and baked rice; half a dozen bowls of mixed and minced meats; two or three varieties of condiments, &c.; then followed a dozen bowls and plates of sweets, cakes, and fritters; and some excellent (white) water-melon concluded the feast. We rather regretted having eaten before leaving our *sala*, for many of the articles on the table before us were quite good—in fact, *very good* when compared with the diet of some of the eastern nations, as, say, the Chinese; most palatable, for example, if likened to the breakfasts, with their *fousty* little bowls of bird's-nest, sea-slug, and shark's-fin soup; unhatched chickens; the stomachs of ducks; fried fat pork, with sugar and pepper; the entire *viscera* of various animals; eggs, much mellowed by lapse of time; putrid fish; and (if one chooses, though they are eaten by the poorer classes only) puppies and rats, which are served 'to order,' in the Mussulman (Chinese) restaurants of Pekin; or even in Canton, where I have seen a sign in an eating-house frequented by well-to-do merchants and artisans—and, by the bye, it proves 'there is nothing new under the sun' even in Yankeedom—which announces to its patrons, in business-like manner, the appetising fact that that desirable delicacy, that luxuriant dainty—'*Best black cats' meat is ready at all hours.*'

A peculiar strong liquor, much resembling camphine, and the Japanese *saki* (rice spirit) less, in taste, was drunk with the dinner; and afterwards we had tea, and then cheroots—native tobacco rolled in palm-leaf and tied with fibre. The serving of the meal was quite amusing. The food was brought in upon silver trays, some of which were placed upon the floor, there not being room for all upon the table. Our plates were of different colour and ornamentation; thus the

General had a red one, the missionary a black one, and I a blue one; and scarcely two bowls or dishes upon the table were of the same size or pattern. We ate with silver-plated forks and spoons, and tried—but miserably failed—to cut our meat with rusty steel knives. The tea was served in brass bowls, from which we dipped with little cups, holding less than a mouthful each. We tried to refrain from laughing, lest the Governor might be offended, but it was rather difficult to keep our features composed when we saw the attendants wiping our knives and forks upon their *pyjamas*, or rending chunks from the general watermelon, and offering them to us in their own hands.

After dinner there was music and dancing, and then the Governor exhibited his gold betel-boxes and other paraphernalia. He told us that all were made by a Cambodian goldsmith in Simrap from the gold and silver coins of Hué, the capital of Annam—of entirely pure metal—and they certainly were very elegant in design and finish. We most admired the cigar case (value $125). The other articles were a large dish which contained the 'kit,' a gold betel-leaf and lime holder; a small gold tobacco-box; a silver cup, with cigars; and a little silver box, made in the form of a fish, containing a perfumed ointment, used by the native noblemen to anoint their lips and nostrils. During the evening His Excellency asked if I would not like to accompany a party of Chinese who were going to Panompin for business purposes; he remarked they were ready to start at once, but, if agreeable, he would detain them until we had seen all the ruins of Angkor. The Governor's kind proposal was accepted with many thanks.

February the 15th was the day appointed for the marriage festival in the palace, but I being sick, my companions thought it imprudent for me to attend. However, in the evening the missionary gave me a detailed account of the entire proceedings. He said that when they reached the Governor's palace the ceremony had just commenced. That they were ushered, amid a tremendous din of gongs, into a large *sala* beyond the reception hall, where were seated the Governor and about a hundred noblemen and invited guests; the bridegroom, a young man about twenty years of age, elegantly attired in silk jacket and *panoung*, was also there. By the time the *farangs* were seated, a procession—headed by the bride, supported on either hand by demure-looking matrons—composed principally of aged or married women, all elegantly attired, entered and slowly marched towards the Governor. The bride was not particularly interesting as regards personal charms; she was young, however, and dressed richly and in good taste. Besides her silk *panoung* she wore a gold-embroidered scarf upon her shoulders, also gold rings upon her fingers, bracelets upon her wrists, and armlets above the elbows. The bride took up her position near the bridegroom, both sitting upon the floor, but not looking towards each other; in fact, throughout the entire ceremony they both were perfectly impassive and *nonchalant*. The marriage ceremony proper now began. A number of wax candles were brought in a salver, and then lighted by one of the nobles. The silver waiter was then passed round before the company eight times, each one in turn saluting the couple and wishing them good fortune by waving or blowing the smoke towards them, thus expressing something like the old English custom of throwing the slipper after a newly-married couple—the band of string and reed instruments playing the meanwhile. Two large velvet cushions having been previously placed before the bride and bridegroom, and upon them a large sword, the leader of the *lacon* (theatricals) now came forward and went through, for a few moments, a most fantastical sword exercise. Dishes had been placed before the unsusceptible couple upon the floor, with covers upon them, which latter the *lacon* man removed during his flourishes, disclosing to view some cooked fowls or ducks; nothing was eaten, however. Next the hands of the expectant couple were bound together, and to each other, with silken threads by the women attendants—probably some near relatives. Thus were they truly 'joined together' in Budhistic wedlock. And this completed the nuptial ceremony.

Afterwards a grand banquet was served in the reception room, the Governor himself officiating. The nobles and guests partook of the viands, sitting apart at little tables by themselves. The *farangs* occupied the place of honour at the end of the hall; and they pronounced the dinner excellent. Several enquiries were made by the Governor and some of the nobles after *Nak Prat* (the 'wise man' or philosopher), alluding to my modest self, for, having learned that I had travelled 'through many lands and over many seas,' they inferred a commensurate expansion of intellect—a large stock of wisdom or philosophy gathered from so extensive observation and study of diverse peoples and countries. Perhaps it is superfluous to add that the term *Nak Prat* was afterwards very frequently heard applied as a surname in our *sala*, until the General and missionary so happily bethought themselves of the necessity of their leaving Siamrap and returning the one to Bangkok and the other to Pechaburi, to reassume the weighty cares of State and Church there separately located. The Governor's answer to the question, 'Where are now the race who built the grand old edifices of Angkor?' was to the effect that a certain king of Siam had pressed these people (whoever they were) so hard that they left their city and fled away off to the north somewhere—perhaps to the provinces of Dangtrong or Tonquin.

The wedding presents of the 'happy' couple were spread upon mats laid on the floor of the reception hall. The Governor's gift was a large lump of gold (worth $450), five silver bars (worth $15 each), an American gold watch and chain, a gold tobacco-box, and 800 silver *ticals*. Upon one mat were 2,000 *ticals*' worth of money in coins of different values. The other gifts were *panoungs* and native trinkets and jewellery.

Late in the afternoon we returned to our *sala* at *Naykon Wat*, and prepared to visit the city of Angkor and its environs.

CHAPTER XIX.

THE RUINS OF ANGKOR—THE CITY AND ENVIRONS

Angkor, styled by the natives *Naykon Thôm*, the Great City, is situated about two and a half miles north-west of *Naykon Wat*, and a good road leads there, through dense forests of immense oil and *poh* trees. Angkor is supposed to have been the capital of the ancient kingdom of Khamen, though we know little or nothing of its history. There is a tradition preserved which sets forth, in most extravagant and improbable manner, that the kingdom had twenty kings who paid tribute to it; that its army consisted of 70,000 war elephants, 200,000 horsemen, and 5,000,000 foot soldiers; and that its 'royal treasury occupied a space of more than 300 miles.' The ancient city was two and a half miles in length and two and a quarter miles in width, surrounded by three walls, the outermost of which, the natives say, it would require an entire day to circumambulate. The outer wall is the only one now at all preserved. It is about twenty feet in height and ten in width, built of large square blocks of volcanic rock, and has two gates upon the eastern side and one upon each of the others. We entered by the south gateway—a pyramidal structure, perhaps fifty feet in height, rising above a pointed arch. On the top of this gateway was growing a *poh* tree, with a trunk as much as three feet in diameter, sending its roots down through and over the huge blocks of stone into the rich earth. The area within the walls is now mostly overgrown with jungle. About a mile north from the gate is a colossal statue of Budha, formed of large stones, and evidently of modern fabrication.

A little farther on, in the midst of the forest, there are the ruins of a large *wat*—a one-storey building, enclosed within high walls, surmounted by twenty-five stone pagodas disposed in parallel rows. These pagodas are about fifty feet in height, except the centre one, which was originally at least a hundred, and the exterior of each is worked into colossal faces of Budha—eight feet long by four in width — upon the four sides. These faces wear a pleasant, good-natured expression, which is heightened by the corners of the mouth curling upwards; the ears are long and narrow, and slit like those of the Burmese Gaudama, but a rather fancy tiara or head-dress takes the place of the short curls of most Budhas. One of these faces is nearly concealed by a network of the roots of the *poh* tree which has grown up from the side of the pagoda. To the *poh* trees is due in great part the present ruinous

WOODEN IDOL.

state of this *wat*, for, having sprung up near or on the tops of the pagodas, they send their roots down through the joints of the stones, forcing them out of place, and, besides, the wind, blowing against their thick and widespread foliage, works almost like a lever upon the roots. Around the bases of the central pagoda are numerous small idol-cells, and there are some female figures carved upon the doors of these cells which are surely of Hindoo origin; besides the corresponding features, they wear the long *sarong* and the round anklets of that nation. It is doubtful if these grand monuments can defy time much longer; some of the blocks of stone in the pagodas are separated by as much as an inch; many seem only to require a touch to topple them to the ground; some chambers are entirely choked up by their roofs having fallen, and over and through all the ruins the parasitical *poh* tree has spread its roots and reared aloft its glossy green head (we saw a solid block of stone, ten feet in length, which was supported in a nearly horizontal position solely by the roots of an immense *poh* tree, grown interlaced around one end of it), and shrubs and coarse grass now riot where once the praises of the great Budha—' the Illuminator of the World '—resounded through the halls.

About half a mile from here we came to the palace gate of the inner or third wall, upon one side of which, on an immense stone platform, rests the statue of the Leper King—he who is supposed to have founded, or at least to have completed, the building of Angkor. The sides of the platform are faced with slabs of stone carved with different featured and costumed figures, all sitting in cross-legged positions. On the opposite side of

THE LEPER KING

the gateway are pictures in stone, a battle and a military procession. The famous statue of the Leper King is carved from sandstone in a sitting posture. The body, which is naked and rather rudely cut, yet exhibits a marked contrast to the physical type of the present race of Cambodians; the features are of a much higher order—indeed, the profile is quite Grecian in outline—the eyes are closed; a thin moustache, twisted up at the ends, covers the upper lip; the ears are long, and have the immense holes in their lobes peculiar to the Burmese and Siamese Budhas; the hair is thick and displayed in curls upon the head, the top of which is surmounted by a small round crown. There is an inscription in ancient Cambodian characters upon the front of the pedestal. The figure of the king is somewhat mutilated; the fingers and thumb of the right hand are wanting, three toes of the left foot are missing, and a large piece has been broken from the left arm. The natives have, with (for them) astonishing forethought, placed a small grass thatch over this statue. They have somewhat naturalised (if a foreigner) and very much travestied their royal ancestor (if indeed such he be) by blackening his teeth, rouging his lips, and gilding his forehead. The precise history of the Leper King has not been determined. There is one legendary tradition that Angkor was founded in fulfilment of a vow by a king who was a leper. Another tradition says that to an Egyptian king, who for some sacrilegious deed was turned into a leper, must be ascribed the authorship of Angkor.

The old city besides, as has been already mentioned, is said by the modern Cambodians to have been built by the angels or by the giants, or to have sprung up from the ground. But all these explanations and the traditions as well are most vague, uncertain, and unsatisfactory.

Agreeably to the legend referring the founding of Angkor to an Egyptian king, and some fancied resemblances between the religion of Budha and that of ancient Egypt, a late writer in the 'National Quarterly Review' (Vol. XXVI. No. LI. art. 'Siam and the Siamese') seems to think these 'point to the fact that at some very remote period the Egyptians, or a people identical with them, held sway over that portion of the globe which comprises Siam, Cambodia, and Cochin China.' But the founding of Angkor is also attributed, and by the most learned Cambodian historians of the present day, to a Prince of Roma—Roma being placed by them at the western end of the world—while Egypt never has occupied that position in the ideas of any nation. Historical students had for a long time entertained very diverse opinions concerning the origin of Budhism. Some had thought that, excepting Brahmanism, it was the most ancient of eastern religions. Others had supposed that it was the primitive faith of Hindustan, which has been driven forth—on the south to Ceylon, and thence spread towards the east and Further India, and on the north to Tibet, Tartary, Mongolia, China, Corea, and Japan—and superseded by other religions; and the fact that scarcely an individual of that belief can be found in India to-day, with the knowledge of the modern sway of Mohammedanism and Brahmanism there, would perhaps not detract from, if it did not strengthen, such a notion. Pocoeke, the author of 'India in Greece,' imagined that the early Greeks were Budhists. Some had thought that Budhism was eliminated from the gross pantheisms of Egypt and Greece, and a few had even essayed to identify Budha with the Hermes of the ancient Egyptians. The Jesuits would persuade us that Budhism is of Nestorian origin. Traces of this ancient faith have been found in Swedish Lapland, and endeavours have been made to prove Budha one and the same with the Woden of the Scandinavians. But notwithstanding all these conjectures and speculations, Budhism is now generally believed by oriental scholars to have originated in the sixth century B.C.—to have sprung up in Nepaul, a country lying contiguous to India on the north; and 'in fixing this date no further reliance is placed on the canonical books of Budhism than seems to be warranted by evidence derived from other sources, for a Hindoo has no idea of real history.'

It is true that the *prachadis*, or sacred spires, of the Siamese slightly resemble *in form*—but more in purpose, for their 'original design was sepulchral'— the Pyramids, *but there are no prachadis among the ruins of Angkor*. The physiognomy of the Siamese and Cambodian Budhas compares better, that is more correctly and fully, with that of several tribes even now inhabiting the plateaus of Central Asia—beyond the northern base of the Himalayas—than any race yet discovered in Ethiopia. And the notion that the chambers of the Egyptian Pyramids were intended to contain relics of sacred animals, which were worshipped, has been exhaustively discussed and amply refuted by the greater number of learned Egyptologists. The Siamese word *Phra*, prefixed to the titles of their kings, means 'lord' or 'master;' it will hardly bear the rendering *Pharaoh*. And the fact that 'the Egyptians were red-skinned, and the Siamese are a mixture of black, yellow, and white, and there are no vestiges of a red race among them,' seems to indicate that the length of time which has elapsed since the red men were there (Siam) has been so enormous that none of the ruins, if the hypothesis of the Egyptians or a people identical with them (can the writer refer to the Jews?) holding sway over a portion of Indo-China were tenable, could now be standing in such tolerable condition.

Budhism has more striking points of resemblance to Christianity than to any religion of Egypt. An eminent Budhist reformer of the fourteenth century once defined the duty of the different classes of Budhists in the following manner:—

'Men of the lowest order of mind must believe that there is a God; and that there is a future life, in which they will receive the reward or punishment of their actions and conduct in this life.

'Men of the middle degree of mental capacity must add to the above the knowledge that all things in this world are perishable; that imperfection is a pain and degradation; and that deliverance from existence is a deliverance from pain, and consequently a final beatitude.

'Men of the third or highest order must believe, in further addition, that nothing exists, or will continue always, or cease absolutely, except through dependence on a casual connection or concatenation. So will they arrive at the true knowledge of God.'

'What is this,' justly asks Princep ('Tibet, Tartary, and Mongolia'), the distinguished Asiatic antiquarian and orientalist, who first deciphered the ancient *Pali* (obtaining his clue to the characters of that language from inscriptions engraved on a stone tablet, now preserved in the Museum of the Asiatic Society, Calcutta), 'what is this but Christianity, wanting only the name of Christ as its preacher and the Mosaic faith for its antecedent? It is these that the missionary must seek to add.' There seems to be much stronger reason for imputing the founding of Angkor to the Jews than the Egyptians, and more still to some tribe which has migrated from Central Asia at a remote period than to either of these races. But, to return after so long a digression to *Angkorthôm* and the palace gate: the inner wall was originally 11 *senu* in length and 7½ *senu* in width (40 *senu* is an approximation to a mile), and about 20 feet in height, with a low stone coping. There are a few minor detached ruins scattered through the forest, and many heaps of bricks, of which latter the city proper seems to have been built. What remains of the royal palace is a large square structure of pyramidal shape, terminating in a tower, the whole probably 150 feet in height. It is much dilapidated. From the staircase the sandstone facing has fallen away, and the underlying coarse volcanic rock is much worn; the steps were so narrow we could scarcely obtain a sufficiently secure footing to ascend to the top. In a small room near the summit were long inscriptions engraved upon the jambs of the doors in the ancient (undecipherable) Cambodian character. Near the palace there lives a petty provincial officer who has had charge of the ruins, he told us, for over thirty years. His reception room was quite an armoury: in it were several flint-lock muskets; two or three fowling-pieces; some large swords, resembling the terrible Japanese weapons; half a dozen powder horns, from which the powder was emptied at the *large end*; some wickerwork shot-baskets, gun wad cases, &c. The officer presented us with pumelows and bananas, and we had a long conversation concerning the ruins, but, excepting the dimensions of the walls, the old man could give but little information.

About half a mile north-west of *Naykon Wat* there are the ruins of an observatory, built upon the summit of a hill perhaps 500 feet in height. A footpath leads up this hill through the thick jungle. The first indication of any antiquities thereabouts is two immense stone griffins, one standing on each side of the path; and next we pass a small image with the head of an elephant and the body of a human being; it is the elephant-headed Ganesh—the god of wisdom of the Hindoo mythology. Arriving at a small level space, there appeared a 'foot-print' of Budha (of modern make), looking like a gigantic bath-tub sunk in the ground. Two large stone towers stood near the 'foot-print,' whose roofs on the interior sloped gradually, with four carved sides, to an apex. The architecture was very beautiful and quite unique in style. One of these towers we found filled with stone and wood sitting images; the other contained a colossal stone king or divinity of some sort, whose head, hands, and arms had been broken from the trunk. It lay upon its back on the floor, and was evidently of ancient make. Its toes being of the natural lengths, we knew it could not be a Budha (in the latter the toes and fingers are of the same length); besides, the head had four faces, and there were four pairs of arms and hands. It was rudely carved from sandstone, and the features were not different from many others scattered around.

This hill is cut in five terraces paved with stone, and having staircases, each about twelve feet in height, ornamented with stone lions upon their balusters; and at the corners of each terrace are small image-houses. The building is quadrilateral, and covers the entire crest of the hill, there being four entrances; the central spire is now an unshapely mass of large boulders, all overgrown with trees, shrubs, and vines. From the summit we obtained an extensive view of the surrounding country, which was level and for the most part covered with *riant* jungle, there being a great number of oil trees. To the north there extended from east to west a range of low blue hills; to the southeast we could just discern the placid waters of Lake Thalaysap; to the south lay the quaint old town of Siamrap; and to the south-west there was another large lake of bright, clear water. We returned to our *sala*, took a parting look at Nagkon Wat, tiffined, and left for Siamrap.

In the evening we paid a farewell visit to the Governor, who received us at the head of the stairs, and escorted us to chairs in the reception hall. His Excellency told *Nak Prat* that the party of Chinese merchants would start on the day but one following; that he would give him a free passage to Panompin, and order everything necessary to be provided for his comfort. There is no possibility of obtaining an interpreter in Siamrap, so it will be necessary to have recourse to pantomime on this journey; and as no native understands the American culinary art, it will be unavoidable that the *farang* should cook for himself. But having no table service—no plates, knife, fork, spoon, or cup—he took the liberty to request the loan of these necessary articles from the Governor, knowing it would not break up any of his sets (?); for, from those he had seen displayed, there were in the palace scarcely two table articles of like material or fashion. During our interview tea and cigars were offered, and at one time the Governor excused himself from the room to order some cakes and fruit, which were served on silver trays. We thanked His Excellency very much for his kindness—the General offering to return his hospitalities at the Consulate in Bangkok, should he visit the capital—and took an early departure.

The night was excessively cold—we shivered under three blankets apiece—and yet notwithstanding so great changes of temperature—40° in twenty-four hours—the climate is said to be quite healthy, except during, and for some time subsequent to, the annual rains. We arose and breakfasted by candle-light; the baggage was packed in carts; the servants were ready; presents had been made; the elephants were saddled and brought round to the *sala*, and my companions mounted and rode away—but not until there had been a hearty shake of hands, and the pleasantest wishes on both sides—towards the west, on their return journey overland to Bangkok; while I was to remain in Siamrap and start alone on the following morning for Lake Thalaysap, Panompin, and Saigon.

CHAPTER XX.

SIAMRAP TO PANOMPIN

THE DAY was passed in busy preparations for the journey. Some cooking utensils were sent by the *Palat* to the *sala*—an earthenware fire-holder, a large iron stew-pan, two bowls for baking rice; and these, with a small porcelain-lined kettle brought from Bangkok, will serve to cook that third of the stock of provisions remaining yesterday which fell to my share. 'Deng,' the cook, had made five or six loaves of bread, some dried apple-pies, and had boiled one-half of a ham, whilst the Governor offered to supply rice, fowls, eggs, fish, fruit. In the forenoon came my new servant a wild-looking Cochin Chinese boy, with his black hair combed straight back from the forehead and tied in a knot behind the head, and his large mouth stained red and his teeth blackened by constant rumination of the betel cud. Returning from a long walk about the town in the afternoon, a messenger awaited my arrival with an invitation to dine with the Governor. This I accepted, and had a very amusing time, owing to the fact that there was no conversation between us, though there was plenty of pantomime (the interpreters had returned with my companions to Bangkok). Having been escorted to a house without the walls, I was received by His Excellency in a very small room, the floor of which was covered with bamboo mats and whose walls were hung with grotesque Siamese paintings. After blankly staring at each other for some time, and making several futile attempts to express our thoughts by vigorous movements of eyes, arms, and legs—at which we both laughed heartily—the Governor took my hand in his own, and thus we walked, at the head of a large crowd of attendants and nobles, out of the compound, and through the gate of the walled town on to the reception hall of the palace. Here a dinner was served in European style, consisting of soup (genus undiscovered); boiled pigs' feet (very good); boiled pork (too fat); roast pork (rather rich); a mixed stew (contents unknown); a dish of uncertain meat, cooked in an uncertain manner; boiled eggs; baked rice (excellent); sweets, four or five sorts of cakes and fritters (all good); bananas (a little wilted); and tea and cheroots, which closed the repast. The Governor was much pleased with my book of sketches, and recognised many which had been taken in his province and in Siamrap town. But our conversation (?) was so fatiguing that the visit was not prolonged to a very late hour. A present of two dozen eggs, six or eight cakes of sugar, half a bushel of rice, a dozen fowls, and about two hundred bananas was sent after me to the *sala*.

On the following morning, the 18th of February, with a buffalo cart for my baggage, provisions, and servant, and a bullock cart for myself, we left Siamrap for Lake Thalaysap and Panompin. The suburbs of the town extend a long way to the southward; these traversed, we entered upon an immense level plain covered with young *paddy* of a beautiful green colour and some six inches in height; water, for irrigation, being conducted over it in little canals, though this is unnecessary during a considerable part of the year, when the lake overflows this section of country. Two or three miles from Siamrap, west of the road, were the ruins of a lofty stone tower, not as grand or beautiful as those of *Nagkon Wat*. Opposite a low sandhill we came suddenly upon the river, where was a camp of natives and a large corral of buffaloes and bullocks. There were two boats in the river, filled with provisions and cooking utensils, which the men were towing as they walked in the stream; farther down were some more boats propelled in the same manner. We next crossed a boggy marsh, and passing through about a mile of thick shrubbery, over a road much cut up by elephant tracks, we halted at the present terminus of the road, for the swamp prevented farther progress by land; and after patiently—or rather impatiently—waiting for nearly two hours, my Cochin Chinese boy succeeded in procuring a canoe, in which we, with bag and baggage, paddled a mile or so to the place where the lake boats were moored.

There appeared to be no village thereabouts, only a little hut where some Chinamen were repairing or building boats. In the water, moored to each other and to the shore, were about twenty boats of different sizes, built somewhat after the Chinese junk pattern, with huge eyes painted upon either side of their prows; their occupants seemed to be Cambodians chiefly, though there were also many Chinamen. The craft to which I was allotted was about sixty feet in length, ten in width, and four above the water-line, with a house, the sides of plank running fore and aft (except a small platform in the stern, for the steersman), raised about three or perhaps four feet at the ridge-pole. It was built of hard wood, gummed (pitched) on the inner side below the water-line, had two decks, a room with two small windows, about the centre of the boat upon the upper deck, being reserved for my own accommodation; and adjoining it towards the stern there was a room to be used by the boy as a sleeping apartment and by myself as a kitchen and storeroom for the provisions. The roof, made of palm-leaf and covered with stout pieces of bamboo, was so low one could only crawl about in the cabin below, where in the middle of the day the heat was almost unbearable. The crew consisted of three Chinese—two of whom were also merchants and owners of the boat—and two Cambodians, and the remaining Chinaman was simply a passenger like myself; we carried no freight. At a bend in the river, a short distance below our moorings, were more huts and boat-builders. The people on the banks seemed to live by supplying the boatmen with fish and other food. The river was not more than thirty or forty feet wide; its banks were lined with stunted, scrubby trees and bushes, which bore a water-mark four feet above the then level of the stream. After an hour of vigorous use of the pole we came suddenly into the lake, two sides of which (the southern and western) were bounded by the horizon; the water was muddy and a heavy ground swell was rolling. After we had all had supper, four oars were rigged forward near the bows (nearly all easterns place their oars for rowing near the bow), the captain worked with another, holding the tiller with his feet, and then we rowed along the eastern shore until after midnight, when the men moored the boat with grass ropes to a large mangrove tree.

In the morning, going on deck, I found, by my compass, we were rowing up a narrow river *to the northward*, and soon after we arrived at a large village—of a hundred huts—where the men signified we were to remain a single night, to receive on board a supply of rice for the voyage. After breakfast I took a long walk on shore. The village—styled upon the map Campong Pluk—is situated upon an immense sandbank by a little river which here empties itself into the lake. The miserable huts are built upon piles eight or ten feet in height, for even the sandbank is submerged with water during a third of the year. The people, mostly Cambodians, though there were some Chinese, are all boat-builders. There were fifty or more boats, in different stages of construction, lying upon rollers upon the bank. Native tools, though of rude make, still are the same in form and purpose as those used by Europeans; easily recognisable were the adzes, axes, planes, saws, and chisels. These people are not very luxurious feeders, a little fish and rice supplying their every need. As I walked through the boulevard of the village some women were weaving with primitive looms the coarse cloth from which their sole and 'confidential' garment is made; in a small temple was an ancient stone image with four arms; near it was a boat, over a hundred feet in length, cut from a single tree. The villagers were most curious; wherever the *farang* stopped a great crowd collected at once around him, and quite a large procession followed him during his entire walk: many natives, doubtless, had never before looked upon a 'pale-face.' The crew of my boat had been on shore all day preparing for the voyage, and in the evening came to ask that they might remain another day, in in order to pound their *paddy* (i.e. remove the husks); this was refused, for ample time had been allowed them; and, besides, the Governor of Siamrap had assured the *farang* he would not be detained anywhere.

At Campong Pluk another Chinaman joined us as a passenger. When we reached the lake, the wind being against us, the boat was speedily lashed to a tree. I suggested the propriety of tacking, as the wind was not what sailors term 'dead ahead,' but the only satis-

faction received was the reply that the boat would
upset, and, upon second thought, I believed the old
lumber-raft would do so, for its bottom was quite
round and had no keel, and the 'house' made it very
topheavy, especially as there was no cargo. In the
evening the mast and sail were prepared for the
expected fair land breeze. The mast was about
twelve feet above the roof of the cabin; the sail was
lateen-shaped and made of mats. The land breeze
sprang up about nine and continued all night, we
making from two to three miles an hour.

The great lake of Cambodia styled *Thalaysap*—the
Sweet Water Lake—is intersected about the centre of its
northern half by the 13° of lat. N. and 104° of long. E.;
it extends north-west and south-east. Its dimensions
are ninety miles in length, twenty-two in width at the
widest part, and eight in the narrowest; its depth is not
uniform; six feet would perhaps represent the average,
although in some places, as in the middle, no bottom has
been found. In the rainy season its length is increased
to upwards of 120 miles. The colour of the water
is a dirty yellow, produced by so many small streams
emptying themselves into it. Current there is but little
in the most southerly parts, where it discharges its
waters into the Mesap river. In the rainy season terrible

storms are sometimes experienced, but during the remainder of the year there is usually an immense fleet of fishing smacks, which cruise about the lake. Thalaysap is fed by one large and two smaller rivers at its northern extremity, by a large stream on the east, and a small one on the west side, and doubtless by many springs and the natural drainage of so low-lying a district. The northern half of the lake is owned by Siam; the southern belongs to Cambodia, which kingdom formerly possessed the greater part of the surrounding region. It was in the year 1795 that the then ruling king of Siam took possession of the provinces of Battambong and Siamrap, as a reparation for some services he had rendered the prince of Cambodia—protecting him from his revolted subjects and causing him to be crowned at Oodong, the old capital.

On the 22nd we passed the boundaries of Siam and entered Cambodia. The wind was usually ahead during the day, but changed in our favour at night. A little of the western shore, or rather side, of the lake was visible, though there was no land to be seen— nothing but reeds and low, scrubby trees. We saw several boats like our own sailing slowly along up the lake. We passed a long series of islands, or what would probably be islands later in the season; they were then little more than distinct clumps of trees. Boat life in Cambodia is rather monotonous where one has no *compagnon de voyage*, and cannot speak the language of the people, and there is no other language understood in common. There is no place to walk; there is no awning or shelter so that one might sit upon deck, and the only recourse left is to lie in bed and read, or sit bent double—for the deck (the roof of the cabin) will not admit an erect sitting posture—and write. However, with reading, and writing, and mapping (at present there are no corect maps of that little-known quarter of the globe in existence, and on the best map procurable I found some of the towns placed as much as thirty miles out of position, and rivers whose entire course varied from three to twelve miles from their real place), completing my rough sketches, writing letters, and *cooking*—I became quite an expert after a week's practice of the latter—I contrived to instruct and amuse myself, and pass during the day the slow revolving hours away. The moon was nearly at the full, and so the evenings were usually passed upon deck, lying on my blanket, smoking a banana-leaf-covered cheroot of native tobacco (made by the Cochin Chinese 'boy'), gazing at the stars, listening to the nasal, monosyllabic utterances of the Chinamen and the equally intelligible blowings of huge fish, whistling for simple company's sake, and ever thinking, thinking of the dear friends then so far away.

One night, when retiring to my mosquito-netting-enveloped mattress, there was perceptible a strong smell of burning punk, and looking into the men's cabin, I found a bunch of joss-sticks smoking before a large piece of red paper, covered with Chinese characters, which was posted against the side of the boat; there were before it also offerings of cake and fruit and a long string of varicoloured papers—*wishes*, no doubt. This may have been part of the 'ancestral tablet' worship, so much esteemed and so faithfully performed by the Chinese, or it may only have been supplications to the divinity who is supposed to preside over navigation—ships and merchandise—for another bunch of joss-sticks was also burned at the prow every evening. We had kept steadily on our course to the south, now sailing, now drifting, now rowing, when at last we perceived a slight favouring current, and we passed several grass marshes and many rows of fish-poles, until, almost without knowing it—for the lake had narrowed so gradually, and so little changed was the appearance of the country—we had entered the river Mesap, which flows past Panompin, and just below that city mingles its muddy waters with those of the great Mekong river. The Mesap was then about a mile in width; the banks were below water and covered with the densest forest.

We sailed by several villages, averaging ten to a

BANKS OF THE RIVER MESAP, CAMBODIA

hundred huts each. Before these were large platforms used for drying fish, and there were also long rows of poles for hanging nets upon. As we proceeded south the banks of the river became higher, and we saw large towns; one of them, built upon a bank thirty feet above the water, must have contained as many as five hundred houses, that of the governor and some others being superior in outward appearance to the majority met with in Siam. One day we saw some natives hauling a net about five hundred feet in length; the inside of the net was perfectly alive with fish of every size, some of them being large. Many towns seemed devoted exclusively to the fish business—drying and salting fish, and manufacturing fish-oil. Some of the fish caught in this river are eight or ten feet in length and three feet in thickness. Immense quantities of fish are caught in Lake Thalaysap and the Mesap and Makong rivers, and being smoked and salted are exported to almost every country of Asia. From the heads of the largest variety fish-oil is made, and from their bodies the condiment so highly prized by the Siamese, and styled by them *namphrik*. These fishing towns occur every four or six miles, and seem to consist of but a single row of huts, facing the river. The first *wat* seen in Cambodia resembled those of Siam; there was a large image-house and a pyramidal tower or spire. We passed the mouth of a small river upon which, fifteen miles from the Mesap, the Cochin Chinese boy signified to me, was the large town or city of Oodong, which was the capital of Cambodia until within the last three or four years.

The banks of the river afterwards became very high, and were cultivated in many places with melons, cucumbers, salad, &c. The river was full of huge nets, the bamboo floats of which were so thick that we had to use the greatest caution to avoid them, the current also being strong. The forests became quite thin, a great number of the trees having evidently been appropriated for firewood. The heat increased; the nights were close and uncomfortable and mosquitoes in myriads abounded. And so we went on until the 25th inst., when we reached the city of Panompin, situated upon the right bank of the Mesap river—here half a mile in width—in about lat. 11° 30′ N., and long. 105° E.; but the rare and varied sights of this day must be recounted in other chapters.

CHAPTER XXI.

PANOMPIN

THE general appearance of the city of *Panompin*— Mountain of Gold—is dull, nothing breaking the uniformity of its bamboo huts excepting a slender, pyramidal pagoda, one of the palace buildings, and two blocks of brick stores, recently built by the King; it resembles many of the villages along the banks of the Mesap, only differing from them in size—in number of dwellings and shops. The water in the river was very low at the time of my visit, and thus the city seemed built upon a bluff fully thirty feet in height; there were no floating houses to be seen, and not a great number of boats, most of which were owned and manned by Chinese. Part of Panompin, to the south, is built upon an island, and nearly opposite this the river which drains Lake Thalaysap—the Mesap—enters the great Makong, one of the largest rivers of the world, which rises near the confines of Tibet, and, after a course of 1,700 miles, empties itself into the sea at the southern extremity of Cochin China, and which at a distance of over 200 miles from its mouth is three miles in width. Another and not a small portion of Panompin is built upon the opposite side of the river, to which ferry-boats are continually crossing. As we sailed slowly down the river, the first objects that attracted my attention were the small but neat buildings—chapel and schools—of the Roman Catholic mission. Next we passed an old dilapidated steamboat, and back of this, on the shore, waved the national Cambodian flag—blue with a red border, and emblems of peace and plenty in the centre ground. Then came the barracks, where are stationed a company of French troops, and the residence of the Commandant, or *Protecteur*, as he is styled, who represents French interests *versus* His Majesty's. Anchored in the stream, opposite the Commandant's residence, was a small gunboat, with a huge tricolour floating from the stern, another from the jibboom end, and still another from the captain's gig; there could surely be no mistake about the nationality of this craft. Further down the river could be seen a brig, a war steamer, and a small despatch boat; these were anchored abreast of the palace and belonged to the King.

Landing near the barracks, I went thither in search of an interpreter—some one who could perchance speak English. My meagre diction was fortunately understood, and a Cochin Chinese boy was sent with me to a store near at hand, where a native of the Isle of Jersey, named Edwards, received me kindly; offered to 'put me up' and to render me besides any assistance in his power. Edwards' house was simply a large shed divided into four or five rooms, only one of which, however, was occupied; the walls of this one—at once sitting, dining, and bedroom—were embellished with fowling-pieces, revolvers, powder-horns, &c.; the sideboard supported an immense array of brandy, claret, and beer bottles—empty ones for the most part—and a small table in one corner was covered with Crimean shirts, hats, shot-bags, boxes of caps, old newspapers, and pipes in endless profusion and confusion. My baggage was brought from the boat and deposited in one of the rooms, which evidently had not been swept or cleaned since the erection of the building at a remote epoch. Some planks placed upon a couple of 'saw-horses,' and my mattress laid thereon, made a bed—and what more could one expect in Central Cambodia? Edwards appeared to be a clever, good-natured, warm-hearted fellow. He had been a sailor, was many years in the Hong Kong and Calcutta trade, and had been in Panompin but a year and a half. He had a very pretty Annamite wife, who was also at the same time his cook—taught by himself. In the afternoon a friend staying with Edwards kindly offered to procure for me an interpreter and to guide me to the Prime Minister's residence.

At two o'clock we started forth, taking the main street, south, towards the palace. The city extends along the bank of the river for a distance of about three miles, and perhaps not more than half a mile at the farthest into the interior; on that side there is a low embankment of earth, erected recently—at the time of the Annamite trouble. There is no wall about Panompin, not even around the palace. The main road runs north and south along the river; there are a few cross-roads, but this is *the* street. It is about thirty feet wide, macadamised with broken brick and sand, and lined throughout its entire length with little bamboo shops, the greater part owned by Chinese, many by Klings, and the remainder by Cambodians and Cochin Chinese. Many of these shops are 'gambling hells;' some are used by opium-smokers; the Klings offer for sale miscellaneous European goods, and the Cambodians silks and cottons: the Cambodians are celebrated for their manufacture of silk. The population of Panompin is about 20,000, and embraces Chinese, Cochin Chinese, Klings, and Siamese, besides Cambodians. As we walked along, the street was crowded with natives. The Cochin Chinese were easily distinguishable from the Cambodians by their height, which is less than that of the latter; their frame, which is usually not so muscular; by their features, which incline more to the Mongolian cast; and their manner of wearing the hair long and fastened in a knot or twist behind. The Cochin Chinese women were clothed in gowns which descended to the knees, and they seemed to be much better-looking than Siamese women.

We called first upon the favourite interpreter of the King—a native of Manilla, named Miriano, who spoke English very well — to engage his services in the expected interview with His Majesty. We next visited the chief aide-de-camp of the King—an English Jew—and found him busy trying on a new military uniform—covered with an enormous amount of gold lace, and with a pair of gilt epaulets fit for a field marshal—which he had had made in Hong Kong, to be worn during the approaching *fête*. It appears that about ten days from now a grand *fête* is to be celebrated in Panompin, on the occasion of the hair-cutting of the

Princess, daughter of the King, upon her coming of age. His Majesty is making grand preparations for this *fête*, intending to eclipse all past attempts of this nature in Cambodia or even in Siam. The officials and many private individuals of Saigon are invited to be present and take part in the ceremonies.

Leaving the house of the aide-de-camp, we proceeded to that of the Prime Minister, who is a brother of the King. His dwelling and grounds are pleasantly situated upon the bank of the river near the centre of the city, and present a decidedly European aspect. The audience or reception hall is about sixty feet long by thirty wide, and extends upward to the tile-covered roof. The floor is covered with fine matting; two or three cane chairs stand upon one side; the walls are adorned with about twenty looking-glasses and a dozen engravings rather fitted for a bar room; upon each of the centre posts are clocks—four in number, only two of which, however, were going. The front of the reception hall was open, and was approached by three flights of stairs; the garden in front was filled with beautiful flowers and plants. Sending in my letter from the Governor of Siamrap, the Minister soon appeared, and after the customary salutations sat down, broke the seal, and commenced to read it aloud.

He was an old gentleman, well preserved—the affairs of state probably not demanding any great physical sacrifice—and he was clad in nought but a cotton *panoung*. We had no interpreter, but understood the Minister to imply that at five o'clock I could obtain an audience with His Majesty. Returning to Miriano's house, my friend left me, and then the interpreter and myself proceeded to the palace.

As already mentioned, there is no wall around the palace buildings, but one is to be built as soon as possible; the exterior limit of the royal abode is at present marked by a simple row of brick barracks upon the front side, which faces the river, and bamboo huts upon the others; the wall will be, when built, about a quarter of a mile square. There is an open space, perhaps five hundred yards in width, which extends around, but from without little can be seen excepting the roof of the new ambassadors' audience-hall, the palace, and an artificial hill now building for the *fête*. We entered by a private side gate—for access to the palace enclosure may be had at all times—and saw before us the unfinished hill; but I was hardly prepared for the scene presented to my eyes in respect of the palace. Imagine in a Cambodian town of bamboo huts, if you can, a two-storey and a half

brick and stucco house of the most modern and
elegant construction, with a double-walled entrance
and columned verandahs, painted yellow, with white
borders and trimmings. Manilla men, with glistening
muskets and swords, were standing on guard in the
vestibule as, preceded by the interpreter, I ascended
the marble steps, passed through a crowd of prostrate
nobles and along a paved hall, the ceiling and walls of
which were beautifully frescoed, the latter bearing, in
bright colours, the crown and royal cipher 'N.'—for
'Norodom I.,' probably after the western Napoleonic
style, for since the King has become a French
protégé he imitates France in everything.

CHAPTER XXII.

AUDIENCE WITH THE KING OF CAMBODIA

In a room about the centre of the palace, at a small round table, sat the King, a pleasant-looking person—thirty-six years of age, as he afterwards told me. He was a little man with intelligent and expressive features; teeth blackened from the use of betel, wearing his hair after the Siamese fashion, the head shaved excepting a small tuft upon the crown; upon the lip was a thin moustache; and he was dressed in a white linen jacket, with gold buttons, and a silk *panoung*, his feet were bare, and around his neck was a fine gold watch chain, upon which were strung some rings, one or two of them set with very large diamonds. Upon the table was a most elegant and valuable set of frosted and engraved gold vases, betel and tobacco boxes, cigar-holders, bottles, and pomade boxes; some large atlases and superbly bound albums, two volumes of a pictorial history of England, a red cloth military cap very heavily embroidered with gold thread, and some curiosities. I conversed with the King, through the interpreter, for upwards of an hour, principally concerning Burma and Siam, though the subjects of Panompin and Cambodia were also introduced. His present Majesty is a son of one of the brothers who, in the last war which Siam had with Cambodia, were retained in Bangkok as hostages or sureties for the good behaviour of the reigning monarch. And having been born, brought up, and educated in Bangkok, His Majesty knew very well many of the people I had had the pleasure of meeting there. The King seemed much pleased at my telling him his palace was superior in every respect, excepting size, to that at Bangkok (though the new palace now being built in the latter city will probably be, when completed, the most splendid edifice of the kind in Asia); it seems to be his great desire to excel the King of Siam in everything.

After asking my age, nationality, and business (stereotyped questions in the East), the King remarked that I had fortunately arrived at Panompin in time to witness the greatest *fête* ever celebrated either in Cambodia or Siam, that he was himself to perform the religious ceremony of cutting the hair of his royal daughter on the summit of the artificial 'mountain' then in process of construction in front of the palace. His Majesty told me that last October he, in company with the French Governor of Saigon, had visited the ruins of Angkor, and that he was very much astonished at their grandeur and beauty; he believed that Angkor was built 1,400 years ago. My present to the King was a fine gold-mounted revolver, in a case with proper appurtenances, and a large brass box of cartridges. In return His Majesty said that if there was anything in the palace or city which I wished, it was only necessary to acquaint him with the fact to possess it; this was rather obscure and equivocal, so I merely bowed in reply. He desired me to come and see him whenever convenient, at least twice before leaving, if I did not determine to remain for the *fête*, and in the meantime he would think of some gift for me as a keepsake from himself. Seeing me peering rather curiously into some of the adjoining rooms, the King asked if I would not like to look through the palace; the foreigner was only too happy, and His Majesty graciously led the way into the parlour.

The palace is but just completed. It was planned and its erection was superintended by a French architect, but it was built throughout by Cambodian workmen. The construction and furnishing is thoroughly

European in nearly every part. Entering at the grand central door, the hall leads direct to the reception-room, and this opens into the parlour. Upon the right of these rooms is the dining-room, and upon the left the library, staircase, and billiard-room—Billiards? Yes, verily, and the King of Cambodia plays a 'good safe game.' In the rear of this building are the apartments of the harem, and not at all ill-looking were many of the saffron-powdered damsels the stranger chanced to espy. The ceiling and walls of the parlour were frescoed in as fine style as many in Grosvenor Square or Fifth Avenue; upon the floor lay a velvet carpet; the window frames held panes of stained glass; upon a large bow-window were the King's arms and name—Ong Somdetch Norodom Phranarowdom—and below the word 'Campuchia' (Komphuxa, or Cambodia). The walls were hung with elegant mirrors and paintings; upon the marble-top centre table was a set of gold chewing (betel) and smoking apparatus; upon side tables were costly clocks, barometers, Chinese and Japanese carved ivory goods, bronzes and vases; and from the ceiling depended a beautiful chandelier. There is, however, no gasometer yet working in P'anompin, but surely it would not be a very long step in advance of the numerous modern importations of the palace.

The dining-room contained black walnut furniture, and upon the side-boards were massive silver table services. On the walls were large steel engravings of 'Napoleon III. at Solferino,' and 'Prince Malakoff at Sebastopol.' Upon one of the tables was a music-box, about four feet long by two in width—a magnificent instrument, manufactured in Paris. His Majesty having obtained the key, wound it up for our amusement. It played eight selections from popular Italian operas in a sort of orchestral style—there were flutes, drums, cymbals, and bells. But the most curious and wonderful part was a bird, about two inches in length, which stood in a small grotto of leaves in the side of the box, and which would turn to the right or left, raise its wings, open its mouth—disclosing the tongue—all in correct time to the music. It was a perfect marvel of mechanical skill, and would bear the closest inspection. This bird was covered with fine feathers of natural hue, and no joints could be detected even when it turned its head. Thinking it might prove an interesting novelty, I showed the King the calendar—dials of the days of the week and of the month—upon my watch; but he had one of that kind, he said, and having fetched it, strange to say, the watch was made by the same firm in Geneva as my own. But there were *some* improvements other than mine possessed, and *some* differences in their mounting. The King's watch told also the month and the stages of the moon—new, full, and the quarters—and was besides a repeater. The cases were most elegantly jewelled; upon the front was a row of large pearls round the rim, and within this circle was the crown, composed of rubies, sapphires, topazes, and emeralds, and below the royal cypher N. in diamonds of different sizes; a large diamond was set in the extremity of the 'stem-winder;' the reverse had also a circle of pearls, and within it the coat of arms or seal of His Majesty most elaborately carved and engraved—in low relief—and in Etruscan gold. This watch was made, at the King's order, in Geneva and Paris, and cost 5,000 francs.

We next went into the billiard-room, which was gaily decorated with what might be styled 'rather fast' pictures; upon one of the tables was another gold betel set, one of the urns being nearly of the size of a half-bushel measure and entirely of gold. The Cambodians and Siamese will possess none but the genuine metal. Some of their articles they stain red, others a deep yellow; both are beautiful, and the engraved arabesque work is superb and very different from anything we have in the West. Crossing the hall we next entered

QUEEN OF CAMBODIA AND ROYAL CHILDREN

the library, which is furnished in green throughout; the walls were covered with green paper; the Brussels carpet was of a dark green, and the leather-seated and backed chairs were of the same colour. Upon the walls were large maps of the different continents of the world and fine engravings of Napoleon III. In one corner was a glass case, containing a small collection of books upon general literature in the French language, uniformly bound in red morocco, with the King's arms stamped upon their covers. In another corner was a large geographical globe and some portfolios of maps and charts, and in another a black walnut writing-desk, with proper *matériel*. A magnificent bronze clock adorned the mantelpiece, and upon the centre table, besides large piles of books and a student's lamp, were two marble statuettes—busts, the one of (wonders will never cease) Goethe and the other of Schiller. The King seemed to take much pride in calling attention to various articles in this room, though he probably understood their uses or applications less than the contents of any other room of the palace.

His Majesty then led the way upstairs, where the rooms were of the same size and arrangement as those below. The parlour and sitting-room were but little

less elegantly furnished than those on the first floor.
Two of the rooms contained small glass cases, in which
were placed gold and silver *fête* and dinner services
and the European cut-glass dinner sets; they were furnished with marble-seated sofas, clocks, and mirrors,
and the ubiquitous gold betel and tobacco utensils. The
two remaining apartments were used as bedchambers:
that of the King was rather plain in its furnishing; the
bedstead was of black walnut, similar to our own; the
pillows only were different, being little, hard, square
bags, with gold-embroidered ends. The King presented me with a small lace bag, which contained, he
said, a dozen different kinds of flowers, and with similar
ones his bed was always perfumed, after the Cambodian fashion. The toilet service was of gold; the
floor was covered with matting, and a few engravings
hung upon the walls. The other bedroom was similar
in contents, except that some of the pictures were
rather plain-spoken; the toilet service of this chamber
was silver, manufactured in European style. Then we
all went up to the observatory, where a small telescope
is mounted, and stepping out upon the roof enjoyed an
excellent view of the river and adjacent country; but
little of the city, however, could be seen, owing to the
dense vegetation. An iron ladder leads to a small

platform still higher. His Majesty did not wish to ascend, but the interpreter and myself mounted, and were rewarded by a little more extended view. While upon the roof the King reiterated again and again that in building this palace he only and solely wished to surpass any edifice of like nature in the city of Bangkok, and it must be admitted he had succeeded.

The strong contrast between the bamboo huts of the city and the grandeur of the palace is painfully apparent, and for the expenses of beautifying the latter His Majesty is said to appropriate private property without indemnification. Still the King deserves great credit for his remarkable energy, his adoption of European ideas and notions; notwithstanding he is said to despise his subjects now he no longer fears them, to mock at Budha when he is in the mood, and to tread under foot the ancient etiquette. Norodom has reigned now for about eleven years, and his rule has been in the main just; he is much liked by the people generally, which, perhaps, is as great praise as any ruler could wish or could obtain. Since my visit the King has left his capital and country, and, determined to see something of the great world for himself, voyaged to Hong Kong, and on to Shanghae, and, I

believe, Pekin. Is not progress in the East quite as
rapid and wonderful as in the West?

We descended from the observatory and walked
with the King across the square to the artificial mountain. This was a huge affair, as high as the palace,
built of bamboo and covered with stout pasteboard,
which was coloured to represent the lower section,
stone; the next, silver; and the upper, gold. It tapers
gradually to the top, to which a path winds, sometimes passing through arches, and tunnels, and grottoes,
and valleys, and the whole exterior is covered with
plants of various kinds in pots and boxes, and wooden
and clay figures of men and animals were soon to be
added to its manifold attractions. Upon the summit
is a wooden platform, and here the King, with due
solemnity and ceremony, will cut the hair of the
Princess his daughter. On one side of the 'mountain,'
upon large mats spread on the ground, sat the nobles
and chief men of the kingdom, assembled to meet the
King, who is there accustomed of an evening to confer
with them on matters affecting the public weal or
woe, but at that time on the absorbing topic of the
approaching *fête*. Many of the nobles followed us to
the top of the 'mountain,' and there the King talked
with them in a very jolly, familiar sort of way, smoking

all the while a Manilla cheroot as much as eight inches in length; in fact, His Majesty smokes incessantly— now a green-leaved, now a dry native, afterwards a German cigar, then a Manilla, &c.

ANNAMITE FEMALE.

Returning to the palace, I observed that all the guards—some fifty or sixty in number—were natives of the Philippine Islands. His Majesty had but few troops in commission; these were formerly instructed by a French officer, but he having been dismissed the service for some irregularities of conduct, military affairs were at a very low ebb at Panompin. I then took leave of the King, very grateful for his kind reception. Arriving at Edwards' house, there was awaiting me an excellent dinner, cooked in the French style by his smart little Annamite wife. And afterwards a native cheroot closed a very laborious but intensely interesting day—one that had amply repaid the many discomforts of the boat voyage from Campong Pluk.

PAKHOIUN, THE CAPITAL OF CAMBODIA.

CHAPTER XXIII.

WALKS ABOUT THE CITY

ONE DAY we walked down the main road, past the palace, and turning to the west, soon found ourselves at the embankment which bounds Panompin on that side, and although but a stone's throw from the most thickly inhabited part of the city, still so dense were the banana and cocoa-nut trees that not a house was visible. The parapet of earth is about fifteen feet high, and the same in width, being faced on both outer and inner sides with large bamboo sticks. Upon it are erected the telegraph poles and the wire which runs from the *Protecteur's* house here to Saigon; there is a branch line from the former to the palace, so that any *surplus* information or *proper* (i.e. for the King to know) news may be sent to His Majesty. But few houses stand without the embankment, and not more than a quarter of a mile distant is the virgin forest.

In rear of the centre of the city, upon a high artificial mound, stands a very old pagoda, some image-houses, small temples, and tombs. The pagoda is the only one at Panompin, and is in most wretched condition. In one of the image-houses was an immense gilded Budha, with mother-of-pearl eyes and finger nails; in another was the large gilded figure of a king, and a lofty four-sided shrine, containing four little Budhas. The pagoda and the great mound were built of diminutive bricks; from the summit of the latter an excellent view of that part of the river upon the opposite bank, including the custom house and the great Mekong river, may be had. There are but two or three priests in charge of the old pagoda; in fact, there are but few priests and temples in Panompin, though the religion here—the Budhist—is the same as that professed by the Siamese. In the evening we went to the palace— there is a stand for musicians near the entrance—to hear the King's brass band. A selection of lively dance music, concluding with the Cambodian National Hymn, was played by the band—Manilla men—of fourteen pieces.

Early on one morning of my stay at Panompin, Miriano, the interpreter, called to offer his services for a visit to some of the public and royal buildings within the palace enclosure. We first looked in at some of the machine shops, where, with French overseers, natives were working a saw-mill and a brass turning-lathe, and where there were forges for making metal vessels and musical instruments. Directly before the palace building is the private office of the King, a handsomely furnished little room where His Majesty receives all visitors on business; behind it are the reception halls, in process of erection and nearly completed. These buildings, built of brick, with tiled roofs and gaily ornamented in the Siamese style, are quite imposing.

The ambassadors' grand audience hall is a room a hundred feet in length, forty in width, and thirty in height, and extending through its entire length are two rows of massive square pillars; the ceiling is to be finished in blue and gold. Not far from this magnificent building is the supreme court—a *sala* open upon three sides, and having at one end, for the King's use, an elegant sofa, attached to which was a patent breech-loading rifle and a Cambodian spear, to be used by His Majesty in case of emergency or necessity for self-protection. There exists what is called 'a board of judges,' but no case of importance can be tried without the presence of the King, from whose decision there is no appeal. Near and parallel to the supreme court is the royal theatre—a large shed open upon three sides, the floor covered with mats, and with a miserably painted scene at one end, though it is not here that the plays are performed, as with us, a narrow gallery just beneath the roof being reserved for the *lacon* (theatricals); a *sala* near by is set apart for the ladies of the harem.

There are several small brick houses within the palace enclosure—the residences of princes, brothers of the King, and some of the higher nobles. In the barracks were about two hundred stand of arms—breech-loaders with sword-bayonets attached. In the King's stables there were three carriages—a barouche, a rockaway, and a buggy—not in very good repair—and a dozen or more horses. Among the latter were two beautiful greys, presented by H.I.M. Napoleon III. It is seldom that the King rides out, owing to the very important desideratum of properly constructed roads.

As previously stated, Panompin has but recently been made a seat of government; until within three or four years Oodong has been the capital of the kingdom of Cambodia. In 1860 M. Mouhot, the French naturalist, visited Oodong, and thus writes of its appearance, which corresponds with that of Panompin at the present day in many respects: 'On approaching the capital the prospect becomes more

WALKS ABOUT THE CITY

diversified; we passed fields of rice, cottages encircled by fruit gardens, and country houses belonging to the Cambodian aristocracy, who come here in the evening for the sake of breathing a purer air than they can find in the city. As we drew closer to the gates I found the place to be protected by a palisade three mètres high. * * * The houses are built of bamboo or planks, and the market-place, occupied by the Chinese, is as dirty as all the others of which I have made mention. The largest street, or rather the only one, is a mile in length; and in the environs reside the agriculturists, as well as the mandarins and other Government officers. The entire population numbers about 12,000 souls [in 1860].

'The many Cambodians living in the immediate vicinity, and still more the number of chiefs who resort to Oodong for business or pleasure, or are passing through it on their way from one province to another, contribute to give animation to the capital. Every moment I met mandarins, either borne in litters or on foot, followed by a crowd of slaves carrying various articles: some yellow or scarlet parasols, more or less, according to the rank of the person; others, boxes with betel. I also encountered horsemen mounted on pretty, spirited little animals, richly caparisoned and covered with bells, ambling along, while a troop of attendants, covered with dust and sweltering with heat, ran after them. Light carts, drawn by a couple of small oxen, trotting along rapidly and noisily, were here and there to be seen. Occasionally a large elephant passed majestically by. On this side were numerous processions to the pagoda, marching to the sound of music; there, again, was a band of ecclesiastics in single file, seeking alms, draped in their yellow cloaks, and with the holy vessels on their backs.'

A telegram had arrived from Saigon stating that the opium steamer, which runs to Panompin, had been chartered by the French authorities to transport some troops to a district of Cochin China where there was a native outbreak; and the regular Government steamer not being due for three days, and then requiring an entire week to reach Saigon, it was necessary for me to leave in a native boat, and Edwards kindly offered to accompany me down the river.

In the evening of the 27th inst. I had my last interview with the King of Cambodia. Upon arriving at the palace about nine o'clock, I found there the royal and some other carriages, and a small escort of cavalry, waiting for the King, who was about to attend a theatrical exhibition, given by some of the great

Chinese mandarins of the city, in connection with the approaching *fête*. The cavalry escort presented a most ridiculous appearance, the men riding without stirrups and clothed in tight black jackets and silk *panoungs*, with blue cloth navy caps, and armed with

GIFT FROM THE KING OF CAMBODIA

huge sabres, carried as nearly as convenient at their shoulders.

After waiting for some little time in the reception room, His Majesty appeared, dressed as a most gorgeous 'swell.' He wore a white choker; white Marseilles vest, with little gold buttons; black cloth frock coat, with flowers in the button-hole; red silk *panoung*; white silk stockings and patent leather

pumps. Around his royal neck was a heavy gold
watch chain, and upon his royal fingers five or six
valuable and beautiful rings; one of them, a diamond
cluster, was a full inch in diameter. His Majesty
was very sorry to hear 'the foreigner' did not intend
to remain for the *fête*, hoped he had enjoyed himself
in Panompin, and said he would now present him with
a little *souvenir*. Thereupon the King sent for his
keys, and opening a huge iron safe standing in a corner
of the hall, took therefrom an extremely pretty gold
pomade-box, and handed it to me wrapped in a piece
of note-paper. This box was made by native workmen from native gold, pure and stained red, in the
shape of a Cambodian pumpkin, the top of which was
carved in a cluster of leaves, and the end of the broken
(purposely) stem of which contained an uncut topaz.
Its workmanship—the engraving, embossing, and
filigree—would delight the eye as well as puzzle the
head (to know how so barbarous a people could
produce such elegant work) of many a western gold
artificer. Thanking the King very much for his
beautiful gift, 'the foreigner' then withdrew. Returning to Edwards', I passed a large open *sala*, where
a genuine Chinese drama—crash, fizz, and pop, similar
to those witnessed in Pekin and Canton—was being

enacted. Before the shed stood the carriage of the King and the cavalry escort, and an immense crowd of people were present, but there was little feeling or excitement displayed.

At one o'clock in the morning we started for Saigon in a native boat, about thirty feet in length and six in width, with five men, who were by turns to row night and day until we reached our destination. The centre of the boat was covered with a low, round bamboo and palm-leaf (very thin) roof or cover—so low that one could scarcely sit upright beneath it—and under this we placed our mattresses and provisions. There were but two positions of body to be had in the miserable craft—a reclining or a sitting—and the passage proved tiresome on this account; and we suffered also from the continued exposure to the sun, the reflection from the surface of the river, the great heat, and last, but anything rather than least, from the mosquitoes.

CHAPTER XXIV.

PANOMPIN TO SAIGON.

We had fairly left Panompin and had entered the great Makong river, which, just below the city, divides into two streams which flow to the south—about fifteen miles apart—and empty themselves into the China Sea. There are many branches and intercommunications— in fact, a perfect labyrinth of canals—near its mouth; one of the smaller streams flows north-east to Saigon, and empties itself into the sea twenty-five miles to the eastward of that city. At first the river averaged about a thousand feet in width; its banks were far from beautiful, being at that season about thirty feet above water-level; the surface was covered with a thick green scum, produced by a species of oil-fish smaller than sprats. On the banks there were few large (woody) trees, but many bamboos, bananas, and betel palms. We passed but few villages, of about a dozen huts each; near them were large patches of cucumbers, melons, and other vegetables; much indigo of fair,

COCHIN CHINESE PRIEST AND ATTENDANT

and cotton of better quality, and *gamboge* (whence the name of the country, Kambodgia or Cambogia)—a sweet-smelling resin which 'exudes from incisions made in the stem of the *Garcinia Cambogia*, a very high tree, the fruit of which is eatable.' Pepper is raised and exported from this section of the country; and the fishing and oil manufacturing is all done above, in the Mesap river and Lake Thalaysap. The provinces along the river are the best cultivated in Cambodia, though the country inland is, for the most part, level and fertile. We met with but few boats. Our course was nearly due south, the current helping our progress somewhat, and the wind also a little—acting as it did upon a wretched sail, about the size of a couple of pocket-handkerchiefs. At night the mosquitoes were so troublesome that sleep was only attainable through wrapping one's entire person in a blanket.

On the afternoon of the second day we entered Cochin China. There is an Annamite custom-house at one side of the river and a Cambodian one upon the other at the boundary line. At Chaudoc we spent part of an afternoon in procuring four additional rowers, knowing that with those we had alone it would be impossible to reach Saigon as soon as desirable. Chaudoc is a town about half the size of Panompin, situated on both banks of the Makong, and also upon a small river which flows west and empties itself into the Gulf of Siam at Kampot; it is laid out with narrow streets, but the houses are not of as good construction as those at the capital of Cambodia. The French have a fort or citadel here, with war stores, about 200 soldiers, and a functionary styled 'District Inspector.' The fort is a simple earthwork, palisaded exteriorly with bamboo, and surrounded by a broad moat filled with water; no guns are mounted, and the whole is in very bad order, being overgrown with trees and grass, the barracks and buildings also within are much dilapidated. The Inspector or his representative, to whom we preferred our request, ordered four men to be sent us; who not presenting themselves within his limit—an hour— he said that if they were not in our boat within ten minutes he should levy a fine of 100 francs upon the village. The threat had its desired effect, for within the prescribed time the men came, and we were able and glad to depart without such an injustice being done the innocent inhabitants of Chaudoc.

About noon, on the 1st of March, we passed a large town composed partly of floating houses, lying on both sides of the river, and called Lang-Xuen. A small French gunboat was anchored abreast of the town, and there was a small citadel, with Annamite troops, French officers, and a French inspector. In the afternoon a small Government steamer, loaded with Annamite troops, passed us on its way down the river, not to Saigon, however. The French Government have about twenty of these little steamers, which are used as despatch boats by the different inspectors, and for transporting troops to the different citadels throughout Cochin China. The latter province or country appeared to be much more thickly settled than Cambodia. The thick forests had given place to very sparse vegetation, and this in turn to large groves of betel-nut, bamboo, and banana trees.

At a large town called Chadec, where we stopped on the following morning, we heard that the opium steamer, already spoken of as being due at Panompin during my stay, had been there, and returning had left Chadec for Saigon the previous evening. We experienced such strong head-winds and tides that it was doubtful if we could reach Saigon in less than a week's time, unless we encountered one of the Government steamers at some of the towns which we passed; and even for a passage on one of these it was necessary to obtain a written permit from a French inspector. Chadec is about the same size of town as Chaudoc, for which it is often mistaken, owing to similarity of the names; there is there a citadel, an inspector, a gun-boat, and some Annamite troops. Going on, the river widened to near a mile, and the number of passing boats, the beautiful little islands in the stream, the large trees and numerous villages upon the banks, produced a very picturesque kaleidoscopic scene.

Notwithstanding a strong head-wind and tide, we succeeded in reaching Mitho, situated upon both banks of the river, and being one of the largest towns in Cochin China, about six o'clock the following morning. There is a large French citadel there, with two or three hundred foreign troops, and perhaps twice as many Annamites. The Intendant's or Governor's residence is a palatial structure, surrounded by pleasure-grounds handsomely laid out with flower-beds, lawns, and neat gravelled walks. Throughout the town are good macadamised roads, bordered with rows of beautiful young cocoa-nut trees. There are several French stores in Mitho; a large brick cathedral is in process of erection; two or three gunboats are anchored abreast of the town; and I noticed several important carriages in the streets. We were now in the delta-ground of the Makong, the land being low and rivers and creeks running and joining each other in every direction. We rowed all day through a narrow creek, the banks of which were covered with jungle; there were no villages, but the creek was full of boats—fishing-junks and sea-junks—the most of them manned by Chinamen. Gradually this creek narrowed to about thirty feet, and our progress was very slow, as it was crowded and jammed with huge rice-boats—some of them with fourteen rowers — salt-boats, fish-boats, and small general merchandise boats, which we had great difficulty in passing.

The next morning, at five o'clock, we suddenly came upon a part of the creek which was entirely blocked with boats, and it being low tide, all were embedded in the mud and could not be moved until the incoming tide should re-float them. Determined not to be thus baffled so near the end of our journey, we took two or three of the boatmen to carry our baggage, and started to walk along the bank of the creek towards a large town called Chalen, which Edwards thought could not be far distant. A walk of an hour, and we were in the heart of the town, and had engaged a *gharry* (we had arrived at semi-civilisation again) to take us to Saigon, about three miles over a good road. Chalen is a very large town, built upon both sides of the river, which is there crowded with boats of every description; it was (and is now almost) the grand terminus of the Makong river and Lake Thalaysap trade, until Saigon, ten years ago but a small fishing village, was taken by the French. The population of Chalen consists mostly of Chinese; the remainder are Annamites, with a few

MAKONG RIVER BOATS

Cambodians. Soon after leaving Chalen for Saigon we passed an immense Annamite cemetery—a mile square of old tombs—simple stone enclosures with small spires, which seem to indicate that there must have been a large city hereabouts at one time, and tradition supports the supposition. Next we passed a few military storehouses, and then some large vegetable gardens, worked by Chinese, for supplying Saigon; and afterwards we entered the straggling suburbs.

We reached the city early in the forenoon, and driving to the 'Hôtel de l'Univers,' there Edwards congratulated me upon the safe, successful, and happy completion of the overland journey from Bangkok to Saigon. I had traversed the great Indo-Chinese peninsula—riding over its plains, voyaging across its lakes, paddling down its rivers—a distance of 655 miles—in six weeks, including many long and delightful delays by the way.

CHAPTER XXV.

SAIGON

SAIGON, captured by the French in 1861, and added to their dominions, together with six provinces of Lower Cochin China placed by treaty under a French protectorate, is situated upon the right bank of the river of the same name, about twenty-five miles from the sea. From Chalen a large creek runs to the Saigon river, joining it about the centre of the city. The approach to Saigon is through an immense forest of the betel and cocoa-nut palm, banana and bamboo trees, and thick copses of others with names unknown, save to the professed naturalist. The first impressions one receives of the town are not at all flattering to its appearance. The only object that attracts the attention is a large three-storey brick building on the bank of the river, at once the town hall and an hotel. In the river, which is here not more than five hundred feet in width, are anchored several small French gunboats— intended for up-country service most of them—and,

STREET VIEW SAIOOX

besides these, there are usually two or three large steamers in port (either one of the 'Messageries,' or an English Hong Kong 'liner,' or one running to Singapore and Penang, or the war vessel of some foreign power); farther down the river are anchored sometimes as many as twenty merchantmen, mostly of five to eight hundred tons burden and flying the flags of either France or Germany.

There are in Saigon very many hotels, or more properly speaking *cafés*, at which the most of the French residents appear to live. These *cafés* are not scrupulously clean; still one may obtain a modest room and fair meals at reasonable charges. The population—ten thousand at a guess—consists of Cochin Chinese, Chinese, Malabars, and French troops, civilians, and a few Europeans of other nationalities. Public affairs are administered by a Governor appointed by the Emperor and sent out from France, and assisted by a Legislative and Executive Council. The streets of Saigon are broad, and macadamised with brick (which makes a very disagreeable dust); in two of them, which run at right angles to the river, are stone canals for the more convenient loading and unloading of the small cargo boats of the country. The street which runs parallel and next to the river is lined with double rows of trees. Here, after sundown, it is the custom of the residents to promenade, while listening to the music of one of the regimental bands. The streets are lighted by oil lamps, and are drained by extensive gutters at the sides. There are no public squares, but there is a small botanical garden, tastefully laid out, but not kept in the best order; in it are some wild animals, among them two fine large tigers, captured in Cambodia.

The public buildings are few in number and not particularly grand in design or elegant in construction, with perhaps the exception of the Government House, recently completed. It is built of brick and stucco, is two storeys in height—about three hundred feet in length by one hundred in depth—and is situated in the centre of a large cleared space on the southern side of the town. The compartments of the interior embrace an elegantly plastered ball-room, rooms for the different offices of Government, an observatory, &c., with marble staircases and balustrades, laid floors, and frescoed ceilings. The appearance, however, of this elegant modern palace, with its grand staircases and pillars, which would appear to advantage in London or Washington, in the midst of a tropical jungle and surrounded only by a few bamboo huts is most droll.

GOVERNMENT HOUSE, SAIGON (FRENCH, RECENTLY COMPLETED)

In one part of Saigon is a large nunnery and chapel inclosed by a lofty wall; there are also many small Roman Catholic chapels.

ANNAMITE MALE

The European business houses are few in number—America not being represented—and trade is anything but brisk. As usual, the real life of the town is maintained by the Chinese, who do the work, keeping small shops of miscellaneous goods generally. The Chinaman is the 'toiler of the East;' he is industrious, persevering, and frugal; his wants are few, and his vices (including gambling, to which he is passionately addicted) never seem to reduce him to a state of beggary. Wherever money is to be made, there you will find John Chinaman; he gradually but surely monopolises the trade and business of all the countries to which he immigrates, and, strange to tell, notwithstanding this, manages to keep upon excellent terms with the lazy natives with whom he lives in contact.

In Saigon there are many schools for teaching Annamites the French language and the general rudiments of education; the children of Europeans are usually sent home to attend school. The army and navy at the disposal of the Governor-General is small, but sufficient to preserve order throughout the French provinces in Cochin China. There is an earthwork fortification at Saigon, which is garrisoned, I was told, by about three thousand men; it contains, moreover, a large quantity of provisions and war stores. The troops wear a blue blouse uniform with leather leggings and a white flat sun-hat (pith or cork); they are armed with breech-loading muskets and sword-bayonets. The navy consists of ten or fifteen light-draught gun-boats (for river guards, and to transport troops to the various citadels throughout the country), the whole under the command of an admiral. The police system is very effective, Malays from Singapore having been enrolled and trained for that service.

ANNAMITE SOLDIERS

Morals are at the low ebb usually found among Europeans in oriental towns—the French living at free quarters with Annamite girls, whom they purchase, when quite young, from their parents, $30 being considered a high price. The climate of Saigon is hot, being so near the equator, but it is generally considered healthy for temperately-living foreigners; the diseases are those incidental to the tropics everywhere—fevers, dysenteries, and cholera in its various stages. The French language is of course that in common use by all Europeans and even by the Annamites, who learn to speak it without much difficulty.

'France in the east' is, as far as my limited observation goes, a great farce—a travesty, a burlesque upon colonisation in general. The French character is sadly wanting in many of the virtues necessary for successful pioneering in foreign lands; it lacks that sturdy, energetic, persevering trait which we see so ably displayed by the English in India and Australia and by the German settlers in America. It must be that politics alone have to do with the retaining by France at the present day of so minute and oddly situated a province as Pondicherry, or such a country as Cochin China, inhabited by so warlike and rebellious a people. After seeing the healthy, growing, and usually *paying* colonies of the British Empire in the east, a visit to Saigon, 'the infant capital of Asiatic France,' leaves a ludicrous impression indeed upon the mind of an observant, thinking, and reflecting traveller.

The great hope of France that the Makong river might prove a water-road and an outlet to the rich districts of southern China, *viâ* Saigon, has proved an illusion, and that geographical mystery has been cleared away with the survey and exploration of the river, nearly to its sources, by a French Governmental commission. An account of this exploration has been given to the world in a book styled 'Travels in Indo-China and the Chinese Empire' by M. de Carné, a member of the commission. And a late writer in the London 'Daily Telegraph' thus sums up the results of the expedition up the great Makong river:—

'M. Louis de Carné started in the summer of 1866 from Saigon, in French Cochin China, to track the great river of Cambodia, the Makong, to its sources. The hope of the French Colonial Office was that this large stream, unknown, like the Salween, the Menam, and the Tonquin, might offer an available water-road through Laos and Yunan to the back of China, and give to the Cochin Chinese delta which is held by France the commerce of a second Nile or Ganges. This hope has failed; the Makong, which the Frenchman traced at the cost of terrible hardships and great sacrifice of brave and valuable life, is an 'impassable river,' broken at least thrice by furious cataracts and having a current against which nothing could be navigated. The discovery, purchased at the cost of existence by the leader of the expedition and by M. de Carné, whose story is posthumously published, takes away half the value of Cochin China. It is our [England's] turn to find out whether the great streams which have their *embouchure* at Bangkok and Maulmain offer any better chance of a back way into the Yang-tse-kiang.'

In connection with a 'back way' route to China, it may be mentioned that the members of the French commission found the Songkoi—a fine river nearly two hundred miles in length, which flows into the Gulf of Tonquin by two mouths—perfectly navigable, and 'in every way fitted to promote the commercial intercourse of the Celestial Empire with our new colony.' Though this could hardly be termed a discovery, for the most northerly of the two branches of the Songkoi, which is about a mile in width at its *embouchure*, is known to have been safely navigated by European shipping in the seventeenth century.

My good friend Edwards of Panompin unweariedly accompanied me about Saigon, acting as interpreter, packing my curios, and assisting me in any and every way he could, and only left me on board the 'Messageries' steamer as the bell rang for all not passengers to leave her decks and their friends for the shore. The Saigon river remains about the same width—500 feet—until it reaches the China Sea; it is tortuous but deep, allowing vessels of the largest draught to steam quietly up to the city. The country on either side is low, level, and thinly peopled; the banks are lined with mangroves down to the very water's edge. At the mouth of the river, upon a low hill, is a lighthouse with a powerful light, and in a sheltered position behind this hill there is a small fishing village where the pilots and their families reside.

We steamed gaily down the tortuous river and out to sea, where we met a favourable breeze from the northward; all was prosperous and hopeful, but as I slowly paced the deck on that beautiful star-lit night of the 4th of March, 1872, I could not but feel sad at the thought of leaving the marvellously beautiful countries and the strange people and stranger customs of Farther India, probably for many years, possibly for ever.

Our steamer was the 'Alphée,' 1,000 tons burden, of the French line; and among others Admiral Dupré, the Governor of Cochin China, was a passenger to France for the benefit of his health. And I was a passenger to Ceylon—to visit in the centre of 'the divine island' the wonderful ruins of structures erected

2,400 years ago—to see the *Lava Maha Paya*, with its 16,000 pillars, the mountain temples at Matate, the grottoes of Dambool, and the Lake of Candeley, with its embankment of stones fourteen feet in length, laid regularly one above the other.

We had a pleasant and delightful passage to Singapore, and thence on to Point de Galle, where I may with some propriety take leave of the reader; for from Ceylon the great and mighty religion of Budha, without doubt, first spread to Burma and other countries of Farther India.

www.ingramcontent.com/pod-product-compliance
Lightning Source LLC
Chambersburg PA
CBHW020301240426
43673CB00039B/662